PETER COLEMAN (right) has a PhD in cultural studies from Monash University, where he tutored in Eastern religion and philosophy. After leaving university, he began a career in the not-for-profit sector, where he now works as a consultant. Peter is also an authorised marriage celebrant and occasional tarot-card reader. He lives in Melbourne with his husband Mike and an ever-expanding book collection.

MATT FOWLES (left) is the co-owner and CEO of Fowles Wine, and the man behind the 'Ladies Who Shoot their Lunch' wine – the world's first wine to have been blended to complement wild game meat. Matt's wines have received international recognition, including the trophy for Australia's Best Shiraz from the Great Australian Shiraz Challenge and a listing in the *Wine Spectator*'s 'Top 100 Wines of 2020'. He currently sits on the board of Wine Victoria. Matt lives in the Strathbogie Ranges with his wife Lu, their three daughters, a dog, a horse, five chickens and a bunch of sheep.

PETER COLEMAN & MATT FOWLES

Weekends with Matt

Published by Affirm Press in 2022
Boon Wurrung Country
28 Thistlethwaite Street
South Melbourne, VIC 3205
affirmpress.com.au
10 9 8 7 6 5 4 3 2 1

Text and copyright © Peter Coleman and Matt Fowles, 2022
All rights reserved. No part of this publication may be reproduced without prior permission of the publisher.

This book is a work of non-fiction based on the authors' conversations, experiences and memories. We acknowledge that some creative licence has been used. Places and timings have sometimes been rearranged. In certain instances, names have been changed and individual 'characters' have played the role of multiple people. While this book is not entirely accurate, all efforts have been made to remain faithful to the truth of our story.

 A catalogue record for this book is available from the National Library of Australia

Title: Weekends with Matt / Peter Coleman and Matt Fowles, authors.
ISBN: 9781922711991 (hardback)
Cover design and internal illustrations by Karen Wallis
Photograph of authors by Colin Page
Typeset in Garamond Premier Pro by J&M Typesetting
Printed in China by C&C Offset Printing Co., Ltd.

To Mike,
Luise, Lilli, Mathilda and Ella,
with love

In wine, there is truth

– Pliny the Elder

~

It dances today, my heart,
like a peacock it dances,
it dances.
It sports a mosaic of passions like a peacock's tail,
It soars to the sky with delight, it quests,
Oh wildly, it dances today, my heart,
like a peacock it dances.

– Rabindranath Tagore

~

Let us be grateful to the people who make us happy; they are the charming gardeners who make our souls blossom.

– Marcel Proust

Contents

Introduction by Matt Fowles   *1*

Chapter 1: Riesling   7

Chapter 2: Shiraz   27

Chapter 3: Pinot noir   51

Chapter 4: Chardonnay   71

Chapter 5: Arneis   91

Chapter 6: Sangiovese   111

Chapter 7: Pinot grigio   131

Chapter 8: Mourvèdre   149

Chapter 9: Cabernet sauvignon   171

Chapter 10: Merlot   189

Chapter 11: Vermentino   207

Chapter 12: Sauvignon blanc   225

Epilogue: The unopened bottle   *239*

Acknowledgements   *245*

Introduction by Matt Fowles

'Wine has the power of filling our souls with truth, knowledge, and philosophy.'

– Jacques-Bénigne Bossuet, Bishop of Meaux

I was drawn to wine at a relatively young age. The attraction was perhaps sparked by wine being served at our family table with friends – typically during some of the more memorable occasions – but, on reflection, I think it was more than that. Wine captured my imagination. I was attracted to the idea of it: the regions it came from, the people who helped to create it, the romance of a life on the land. As I had always dreamt of being a farmer, to me, wine seemed like such a perfect product of agriculture, simultaneously humble and extraordinary.

I know wine is a humble drink. At its essence it is the juice of the grape, plus yeast. Yet despite this simple and fundamental truth, wine has always commanded a particular reverence. This is the 'magic' of wine, to which I was also so strongly attracted.

Why was wine a feature of so many ancient philosophers'

tables? Why has it been used in religious ceremonies for millennia? Why do people travel the globe like pilgrims to visit its various homes? Why is wine as relevant today as it was 7000 years ago? Why are our social occasions and ideas more free-flowing over a glass of wine?

In the chapters that follow, we explore our extraordinary connection with wine, and the remarkable power it has to capture and ignite the imagination.

With so many tricky terms and concepts attached, the world of wine can be intimidating. All the constructed pomp and ceremony can prevent people from simply enjoying the drink. After all, the story behind wine – the places, the people and nature – is a language we all speak. So, if you enjoy travelling, then you can enjoy wine. If you enjoy catching up with friends and family, then you can enjoy wine. If you have ever stopped to smell the roses, then you can enjoy wine. If you listen to music or enjoy art or meditate, then there is a place for wine in your life.

I wish I had had this advice when I started my journey in wine. It would have helped me to pay more attention to its truth, and less to the bullshit that often accompanies it. To be (uncomfortably) honest with you, even after well over a decade in the industry, I am still intimidated by some of the settings, institutions, egos and language associated with wine. But this is not wine – this is a construct around wine. It is, in fact, unnatural to sit in a restaurant adorned with linen tablecloths, fine cutlery and glassware. It is unnatural to describe an agricultural product as 'racy', 'tight' or 'brooding' (although I am guilty of this!). Would you describe a tomato that way? It is unnatural, and unnecessary, for winery owners and salespeople to be competitive with other wine producers about being the 'best'. One of the single greatest things about wine is that it is always open to interpretation. Your opinion is the only one that counts. Wine is what you want it to be.

When I first came to wine, I was a disillusioned young professional in the legal world. Although I had a keen interest in wine, my experience was limited. My training in law had always been to assemble all the information, analyse it and then reduce it to single points of fact. This is how I first approached wine when I joined the industry. I tried to contain it, quantify it and put boundaries around it. This is, of course, impossible.

It is said that 'Masters of Wine' – the black belts of the wine world – can taste a wine 'blind' (without knowing where it is from) and can often trace it back to a single vineyard, a winemaker and the vintage year. They are human wine encyclopedias yet their knowledge will never be complete because, with every season, Mother Nature rewrites history.

Wine is evocative, not prescriptive. There is no start and finish. There is no black and white. There is no end point. Over the years I have learnt to take a more open-minded approach to wine; not seeking to measure it by metric means, but rather to open my mind to the less measurable, the deeper dimensions, the layers and the magic. It is because of this that anybody can appreciate wine.

Once I had learnt to enjoy wine differently, I started to look at life differently. Where previously I had sought to control outcomes, I now relinquished control and enjoyed the ride. Wine taught me to be more malleable and less rigid. To accept people as they are and enjoy their idiosyncrasies. To do more to listen, interpret and feel. To trust my instinct and not rely so heavily on others for advice. To learn and evolve. Wine has the power to open your world in unexpected ways – you just have to give it the chance.

Life sped up for my wife, Luise, and I when our beautiful kids arrived. Balancing the demands of a winery, and a family, can leave little time for contemplation. There are many times when I find myself with a swirling mass of ideas, without the time and space to draw the threads together.

This is where my mate, Peter Coleman, comes in. 'Sweet Pete', as my family knows him, has been a great teacher in my life. He is not the kind of teacher I have been used to in the past; his approach is not so much about imparting knowledge (although he frequently does). He focuses on deep thought and guiding you to your own conclusions about how you might view your world differently. He helps to create space for me to 'draw the threads together', without judgement or seeking to influence the outcome – although he certainly informs it.

Introduction by Matt Fowles

Apart from having a giant brain and the extraordinary knowledge that comes with it, Pete has weighty life experience, giving him profound and deep insights and empathy. Though I have told him how much he has taught me, I doubt he will ever really understand the extent to which his thinking and guidance has influenced my life. He has an uncanny ability to help me (and others) see the world differently. He is the philosophical equivalent of the Masters of Wine, to which his PhD attests.

So, when Pete suggested that we work together on this wonderful book, the answer was an excited 'Yes!' I wanted to explore the magic world of wine, and I knew Pete could help me see it with more clarity.

This book defies a clear category – it's part wine guide, part memoir, part philosophy handbook. Like wine, it is much more involved than it first appears. I hope it gives you fresh insight into wine, life and friendship. I hope it will help you to pause and reflect. I imagine it will help you to 'draw the threads together' for yourself. But above all else, I hope you enjoy it as much as we enjoyed bringing it to life.

CHAPTER 1

Riesling

'Just grab something nice.'

That was the instruction from my husband as I headed for the bottle shop. On paper, it wasn't a challenging assignment. I was a twenty-something, well-educated man living in cosmopolitan Melbourne. I often ate out, had an ample circle of friends, and enjoyed whiling away the hours in candlelit conversation. I should have known *exactly* which wine to pick up for a dinner party.

I had no idea.

I had never taken any interest in wine, or alcohol in general. This wasn't founded on any particular ethic. I wasn't raised in an Amish commune. Alcoholism didn't run in my family. I was far from a fitness fanatic dedicated to 'clean living'. Drinking had simply never appealed to me. The situation was such that many of my friends assumed I was teetotal. I would point out that I didn't *not* drink, in the same way I didn't *not* watch Czech cinema. I wasn't actively opposed to it. I just wasn't going to free up time in my schedule to go to an Eastern European film festival.

I had occasionally wondered if there was some glitch in my wiring when it came to drinking. Other people seemed to derive such pleasure from it. A month earlier, when Mike and I were planning a trip to Canada, I had deliberated with a friend over what present to buy our Canadian hosts. 'Why don't you take them a bottle of nice Australian wine?' she had suggested. 'Everyone loves wine ... except you.' The option of giving wine had honestly never occurred to me.

Well, this *had* been true right up to the point where I was standing in the bottle shop trying to fulfil a duty for which I was woefully unqualified. The first iPhone was yet to be released, so easy access to the internet's wine knowledge was not at my fingertips. The ginger-haired sales attendant was busily engaged with a mildly deranged client. I was at a loss.

I wandered the aisles, trying to make sense of it all. Out of curiosity I picked up a darkly coloured, well-designed box holding a single bottle of Scotch whisky. I read the description. This liquor boasted a 'medicinal flavour' with notes of 'iodine' and 'seaweed'. I imagined a bruised merman being bandaged up after drunken fisticuffs with a hammerhead shark. I was surprised to learn that the taste of salty Band-Aid was appealing to some people. I returned the whisky to its place on the shelf.

Cold, condensation-dripping glass doors displayed green and yellow bottles of white wine. Like a bookshelf of occult manuscripts, the words and designs on the labels spoke an obscure language. The names of various estates, valleys, cellars and vineyards might as well have been written in hieroglyphics. Equally meaningless were the different varieties. Choosing wisely between pinot grigio, chardonnay and sauvignon blanc would have been tantamount to deciding between mystery prize doors on a game show.

I turned to the red wine section. Bottles on top of the shelves were laid out sideways, resting at room temperature. I somehow found the reds more appealing to browse through. The dark glass bottles looked elegant. But as with the whites, I was bemused.

It was the Italian wines that gave me the clue I needed. As I scanned the myriad tenutas, fattorias, villas and castellos, I landed on a bottle of Toscana Rosso. My grasp of Italian was nearly non-existent, but I understood Toscana meant Tuscany. Tuscany … Tuscan wine … talking about wine in Tuscany … All of a sudden, I knew what to do.

I walked outside and phoned a friend. To my relief, he answered.

'Hey, mate! How are you?' Matt asked.

'I'm well, my friend! How are you?'

'I'm great! Congrats on the big news! I'm so happy for you guys.'

It was on our trip to Canada that Mike and I had got married. We were holidaying on Vancouver Island with Mike's best friend Dave. Same-sex marriage had just become legal in Canada and we thought 'why not?' We had kept it a small affair, with only seven in attendance. The day had been for the two of us. We were happy not to make a fuss.

'Thank you,' I replied. 'But before we go any further, this is a crisis call. I have to choose a bottle of wine and I have no idea what I'm doing. You're the biggest wine expert I know. Help!'

Matt and I had met on a study trip abroad. At the time, I was a nineteen-year-old undergraduate student. I was studying humanities and wearing mostly black. I was depressed and buried myself in study. My grades were high, but my spirits were low. Money from a scholarship, support from my parents and encouragement from friends led me to sign up for the 'Renaissance in Florence' course. It promised a month of cultural immersion and history in the birthplace of the Italian Renaissance. I thought that maybe it was the change I needed to break out of the heavy, joyless rut I was in.

Matt had chosen to go on the Florence trip for more inspired reasons than mine. He was studying for a double degree in law and humanities, and had taken a particular interest in Renaissance history. He had never been to Europe before and was eager to enjoy the Italian culture, food and wine. The 'Renaissance in Florence' course was a dream come true.

His high hopes were not misplaced. Florence had been enchanting. Gems of art and architecture were bountiful and breathtaking. Whether touring the Uffizi Gallery, circling the Duomo or enjoying gelati in the Piazza della Repubblica, there were treasures to be enjoyed at every turn. At times it was hard to believe that such a place existed. But what made that trip truly special was the study group itself. We bonded quickly, strangers becoming acquaintances becoming friends in a matter of days.

Matt enjoyed watching me flamboyantly bemoan getting mud on my coat one day early in the tour. He had struck up a conversation. I was surprised he liked me. He seemed the kind of tall, polo-shirted, cap-wearing, law student type who I lumped in with the boys who had bullied me in high school. I was wrong. We got along famously. He would tease me about my crushes on the Italian policemen. He was obviously enamoured of his girlfriend, Luise. He would talk about her at length. He also had an abiding passion for wine, but I was more interested in hearing about Luise.

Five years on, my connection with Matt remained unbroken; in response to my plea for wine guidance, he was at the ready.

'What's the occasion?' he asked.

'It's a dinner party a couple of friends are throwing to celebrate the whole marriage thing.'

Though Mike and I were fine with no fuss, when our friends in Melbourne learnt we had tied the knot, they all seemed intent on making a *lot* of fuss.

'Do you know what kind of food they're serving?' Matt asked.

'Well, they're gourmet types; food and wine enthusiasts. Which is why the pressure's on not to make a dud choice. I think they're putting on a Mediterranean-style, al fresco dining extravaganza.'

'I'd go with riesling.'

The suggestion sparked a faint memory. 'I remember a housemate of mine watching a TV show about wine,' I recalled. 'I wasn't really paying attention, but I think it was some wine expert talking about how much she loved riesling.'

'Was it a Jancis Robinson doco? I love Jancis Robinson. She's a huge fan of riesling, as so many winemakers are.'

'What's so special about it?'

'Riesling is one of the great aromatic white wines. It works in a wide variety of climates and countries and cultures, and always delivers the goods. It's naturally high in acid, which helps it age well. It's very aromatic, which is just so important when it comes to wine. In the Australian show system, they give three points for colour, seven for aroma and then ten points for flavour, which just shows what a big role aroma plays in assessing the quality of a wine. Riesling is an aromatic superstar.'

I had strolled a couple of blocks from the bottle shop by now, and come upon a small public garden. I sat down on a park bench across from a row of cherry blossom trees. They were in full bloom. Fragile pink petals littered the path at my feet. The faint smell of vanilla, almond and lilac hung in the air.

Riesling

Matt carried on explaining: 'The high-acid thing is really important because acid sort of acts like the equivalent of a highlighter pen. It highlights the ingredients in food. So, a high-acid wine like riesling is generally good for food and wine pairing. That's partly why somms are so obsessed.'

'What are "somms"?'

'A somm is a sommelier, a wine expert. They're the guys who recommend the best wine to match with your meals.'

I was vaguely aware that such people existed but had not known what to call them. I liked the word 'sommelier' – it sounded urbane.

'Also, riesling can be made in lots of different ways,' he continued, undeterred. 'You can have a sparkling riesling, you can have a really crisp, dry riesling, you can have riesling that's blousy and round and generous, or you can have sweet riesling in the more German style. There are just so many options.'

Any doubts I may have harboured about Matt's wine expertise had evaporated. He was clearly the right man for the job.

'Another reason that those in the know love riesling is because it's such a faithful conveyor of the wine's provenance,' he explained. 'If you give a glass of riesling to a Master of Wine, they can trace it with extraordinary precision; often to a region, a vintage and even the winemaker, because of how it tastes. Imagine if you could do that when you ate an orange.

Imagine saying "this orange comes from such and such orchard in the Napa Valley". It just blows my mind!'

This struck me as a supernatural ability. Who were these remarkable humans able to use their senses in such a specific way? I was reminded of the novel *Perfume*. Set in 18th-century France, the central character, Jean-Baptiste Grenouille, is endowed with an extraordinary sense of smell. At one point, Grenouille retreats to a cave, spending seven years cataloguing a grand library of scents in his mind. I wondered if Masters of Wine did something similar. Did they construct vast mental wine cellars, ready to pull out the right bottle at any given taste? Did they practise deep vino meditations, sitting in the lotus position with a glass of red and white in either hand?

'I can't believe people can do that,' I exclaimed. 'It makes me think of Proust's madeleine.'

'What's that?'

'It's a little cake, much loved by the great French author Marcel Proust, who featured it in his epic, four-thousand-page-long, seven-volume novel called *In Search of Lost Time*. I've read it, which just goes to prove I'm crazy.'

Matt laughed. 'I can believe it.'

My old friend was used to my wide-ranging literary observations. Almost every flat surface in my home was piled with small towers of half-read and earmarked volumes. It was the standard reaction for any visitor coming to our home for the first time to remark: 'You guys have a lot of books!' Mike and I took this as a point of pride.

'In Proust's novel,' I explained, 'the narrator describes dipping this cake – a petite madeleine – in a cup of tea. When he eats the madeleine, he experiences this sudden rush of memories. The taste of the cake vividly reminds him of eating a tea-soaked madeleine with his aunt as a child. It opens a doorway to memories that not only change the way he sees his childhood, but also his entire life.'

'Wow, that's quite the cake.'

'No kidding. But the way you describe sommeliers tasting wine is kind of like that. They don't just taste wine. They taste places and times. Do you experience wine like that?'

'For sure, particularly if I've been to the place where the wine was made. You can be sitting at home in your lounge room drinking a beautiful Burgundy or Clare Valley riesling, and boom! Suddenly you're there. You can see the countryside and smell the grass and feel the sunshine on your face. You can travel through the wine.'

This was a new way of thinking about the humble grape. I had always assumed people enjoyed wine mainly for its alcohol content. Matt was describing something different. It was more like reading a book or listening to a particularly evocative piece of music. Wine could be transportive.

'Again, I'm reminded of Proust,' I said. 'There's a famous quote of his: "The real voyage of discovery consists not in seeking new landscapes, but in having new eyes." You see wine in a way I don't understand. In Florence, I remember you talking about your love of wine, and I didn't get it. But now you describe the way it brings your memories and imagination to life, it actually sounds pretty special.'

'I love that. But wine doesn't just give you new eyes, as your mate Proust would say. It gives you all the senses anew. When you visit a place, as a wine lover you pay particular attention to things in nature. Things you might not notice otherwise, like the minerals in the soil or the moisture in the air.'

At the time I was a PhD student, studying environmental philosophy. With my dissertation significantly informed by Buddhist and Taoist thought, I was used to having in-depth discussions. But it was nice to speak about ideas with someone who wasn't another PhD student. Those conversations often turned into games of intellectual one-upmanship, littered with words like 'narratology' and 'diachronic'. Speaking with Matt was much more fun.

'Weirdly enough,' he remarked, 'this conversation leads perfectly into some big news I have to tell you.'

I immediately assumed Luise was pregnant. I didn't know exactly how that news would be connected with wine, but drunken evenings can sometimes have unexpected outcomes.

'I'm leaving law,' Matt announced. 'I'm going to become a winemaker.'

Riesling

Growing up in suburban Melbourne, Matt had always longed to be outdoors. He would beg his parents to take him on car rides to the bush. He played with bugs, accumulated pets and took an intense interest in wildlife. Much to his mother's dismay, he would sometimes drag leaf-laden branches into his bedroom as a decorative motif. If Matt couldn't be out in nature, then he would bring nature in.

On school holidays he loved nothing better than to spend time with relatives who had continued the family legacy of farming. These were golden days of youth, spent climbing in hay sheds, mustering cattle, nurturing plants, fishing and even learning to hunt. This was where and when he felt most alive.

As an adolescent, Matt was keen to work in agriculture. However, such a profession was not considered suitable for a graduate of the conservative all-boys school he attended. When he was sixteen, he was told to abandon hopes of life on the land: 'My dear boy, you will pursue a career in either law or medicine.' Matt acquiesced and chose law. It was also at this age that he began to grow interested in wine.

Matt was never a natural student of law, but he applied himself with diligence. He had decided to make the best of the path he had chosen. He studied hard and did well. He applied for clerkships and was employed by a large international law firm. He was excited by the prospect of life as a commercial lawyer – the esteem, the challenges and the opportunities. By sticking with law, he and Luise could travel the world together.

Perhaps they could eventually relocate to London or New York? He would be a well-paid, well-respected professional in a well-fitting suit. He would spend his days in high-rise offices charging for time and ruthlessly representing his clients. He would make his school proud.

The illusion of thriving as a city lawyer didn't last for long. He came to dread his days sitting under fluorescent lights, with the climate control permanently set at 18 degrees Celsius. He felt perpetually dissatisfied and out of place. It was as if the childhood version of himself was lugging branches into his office as a daily reminder – 'You are living a lie.' He hated all the billable hours he spent away from friends and family and his beloved nature. In short, he was miserable.

He began talking with his family about making a change. Then one day his father contacted him, saying, 'I want to show you something that might change your life.' It was an advertisement for a new winery in the Strathbogie Ranges that had fallen on hard times. Matt knew exactly what he needed to do.

My instinctive reaction to Matt's news was to squeal with joy. Stifling this impulse, I replied: 'I'm so, so, *so* happy for you. This is fantastic. Congratulations!'

He laughed. 'So, you think it's the right move?'

'Of course! I never even thought of you as a lawyer. It didn't make sense to me. You being a winemaker just feels right.'

I asked a flurry of questions. Matt excitedly explained the logistics, and his hopes for the future. He wanted to sustainably make industry-leading wine. He wanted to establish his winery on the international stage and for the Strathbogie Ranges to be discussed in restaurants worldwide. I hadn't heard him sound this spirited since Florence. It was like he had woken from a coma.

'It's been great because everyone's been so encouraging,' he said. 'Especially my family. They've backed me all the way.'

'I'm so happy to hear that.'

Perhaps detecting a trace of sadness in my voice, Matt asked: 'Have you heard anything from your folks?'

It had been a couple of years since my relationship with my parents had fallen apart. For a long time, I had led a double life, keeping my sexuality hidden. Things had come to a head one painful Boxing Day. I had angrily stormed out of my parents' house, shouting and accusing. The stress of keeping my secret had become too much. A few days later they discovered the truth – their son was in a relationship with a man. My mother insisted I wasn't really gay. She flooded my email account with 'evidence' to prove that my homosexuality could be 'cured'. I blocked her. Attempts at reconciliation came to nothing. We had stopped speaking.

'No, I haven't heard from them,' I replied.

'Do you think they'll come round?'

'No, I don't think so.'

'I'm sorry to hear that, mate.'

A rush of wind blew past, unleashing a burst of blossom confetti into the air. I thought of the cherry blossom festivals in Japan. In Japanese culture, cherry blossoms (called sakura) symbolise the delicate transience of life, a beautiful reminder that nothing is permanent. I had always assumed that my parents would be a constant in my life. I had been mistaken. The truth of impermanence could be shocking and painful. It could be peaceful, like the annual flourishing and fall of the cherry blossoms. It could also bring the most welcome surprises, like learning your friend had decided to follow his dreams.

I changed the topic: 'How does Lu feel about the move?'

Matt admitted that the change in plans from New York to country Victoria had taken Luise by surprise. She had always assumed that they would eventually move to the country, but the timeline had been brought forward by two or three decades. Having grown up in numerous cities around the world, from Seoul to Vienna and Frankfurt, she was accustomed to metropolitan living. Ever the salesman, Matt had done a banner job of pitching vineyard life. Luise worked in advertising and was skilled at graphic design. Naturally, she would take charge of creating the wine labels and promotional artwork. This was a project she could get behind.

'She's a good soul,' I observed. Matt wholeheartedly agreed.

'Your move to the country reminds me of another famous Proust quote,' I said. '"Always try to keep a patch of sky above your life." I don't think there was much sky above your life as a commercial lawyer. Out at the winery you'll have *all* the sky.'

'I love that. Maybe I should give this guy Proust a read?'

'I somehow don't think you'd enjoy the one-hundred-page-long descriptions of his aunt's daily routine. Proust certainly wasn't afraid of going into detail. Then again, he spent the last years of his life as a shut-in living in a cork-lined room. He had a lot of time on his hands for writing.'

'I think I'll stick to my agriculture books,' Matt said.

I laughed. 'Probably a wise decision. Anyway, back to the original purpose of this phone call. I need some riesling recommendations.'

Matt told me to avoid anything too high in acid. As a beginner, I might find it difficult to drink. I responded that this wasn't the 1960s and I wasn't up for dropping a lot of acid. After politely chuckling at my bad drug pun, Matt listed the names of three Australian winemakers who made excellent, affordable rieslings.

'Thanks so much for the recommendations. I'm so happy to hear your news. I really look forward to taking one of *your* wines to a dinner party someday soon.'

'I can't wait for that either, mate. It won't be long.'

A couple of years later, I had the pleasure of taking one of Matt's own creations to a housewarming. It was a bottle of riesling.

Sitting by the blossoms that day, I took a moment to savour the scene. A smartly dressed woman stopped for a moment to enjoy the blossoms with me. We exchanged a brief smile and she said, 'Lovely, aren't they?'

I nodded in reply. 'Beautiful.'

She smiled again and quietly walked away.

I made my way back to the bottle shop with new-found confidence. I had the names of three commended wines to choose from. I looked forward to explaining my wine selection later that night: 'I thought riesling would be best for bringing out the flavour in the food. Also, the aroma's really pronounced.' Of course, Mike would be quick to destroy the illusion, pointing out that I must have been prepped. It would probably be best to be honest and just admit that I had called in emergency assistance.

Fortunately for the man behind the counter at the bottle shop, the belligerent customer had left by the time I returned. I handed him the list of wines I had written in my notebook.

'Those are some good choices,' he said. 'I'm pretty sure we've got two of those in stock.'

I ended up choosing the more expensive bottle. This was based on the magical thinking that higher cost would equal higher quality. Later, Matt would teach me that this was often a misleading assumption – the price of wine and the beauty of wine were not always synonymous. But that would be a lesson for another day.

CHAPTER 2
Shiraz

Thirteen years passed, and the cherry blossoms were back in bloom.

Matt and I had not remained in close contact. This was not for lack of enjoyment in one another's company. Rather, we maintained the kind of undemanding friendship that is defined by long silences interrupted by moments of immediate familiarity. We would go many months without speaking. Then the phone would ring and anyone listening might have thought we had spoken a week earlier. Unspoken kinship made conversation effortless.

I had watched with delight as Matt's star rose in the world of winemaking. After only a few years in the business, he had been appointed one of the industry's 'future leaders' and joined the committee of the prestigious Winemakers' Federation of Australia. His wines had won numerous medals and trophies. His winery had also garnered multiple tourism awards for 'Best Cellar Door'. His social media was aglow with success, and I was proud.

Matt had also had a lot to celebrate on the family front.

He had married Luise in a beautiful ceremony, and the pair had gone on to have three daughters – Lilli, Mathilda and Ella. Matt was wildly in love with his kids. I had never felt the desire to reproduce, and could not relate to the joys of offspring. Nevertheless, it was gratifying to see Matt and Luise's shared happiness. Matt informed me that the sleepless nights, nappies and toilet-training were entirely worth it, although I couldn't imagine how.

As for me, I had finished my PhD and left academia behind. By the time I had submitted the final draft of my thesis, I was done with footnotes and bibliographies. I didn't even bother going to my graduation ceremony, choosing instead to spend the day at a Buddhist meditation retreat. I sometimes regretted skipping the opportunity to wear the robe and puffy hat that would have been my graduation uniform. Then again, I never looked particularly good in hats.

As fate would have it, I landed a career in charity fundraising. I worked with remarkable, funny, brilliant and eccentric souls. I saw how generous people could be. I was blessed with opportunities to travel and learn. There were ups and down, of course. I took a few wrong turns, made my fair share of mistakes and lost my cool more than once.

Still, there was a lot to be thankful for.

Mike and I remained as steady as we were the day we married. Ours was never a relationship of incendiary passion, but more one of quiet contentment. His calm, kindly nature was the perfect balance for my more dramatic tendencies. We just got along. I sometimes realised how little I would talk about him with my friends. They would ask how he was, and I would reply: 'You know, the same. Mike's Mike. He's the best.'

As for my parents, that was a wound which never healed. Following years of painful silence, I had extended many an olive branch. I sincerely apologised for my part in things – for the hurtful words I had hurled in retaliation to the rejection I felt. I wrote and called and did my best. They did not respond as I had hoped. My mother sent thoughtful birthday and Christmas gifts but did not speak to me. My father spoke to me, but briefly and only two or three times a year. Evidently, time had not altered their views. They never once acknowledged Mike's existence.

Life continued, as it does, and one evening I watched a documentary called *Somm*. The name had caught my attention. I was reminded of the time that Matt had introduced me to the term. The film followed four wine professionals as they prepared for the notoriously difficult Master Sommelier exam. The candidates subjected themselves to a gruelling study regimen to perfect their knowledge of wine and spirits, as well as hone their skills in table service and deductive tasting. Like athletes in preparation for the Olympics, they trained tirelessly in pursuit of their goal. As with the Olympics, there were also winners and losers. When the exam finally came, only two of the four attained the rank of Master Sommelier.

It was captivating to witness the passion of these aspiring 'Masters'. They were not simply pursuing a career or a title. They *really* loved wine. More than that, they found meaning in their relationship with wine and the culture that surrounds it. For them, wine was much more than pressed grape juice – it was a philosophy, a religion, a way of being.

My memory leapt to the conversation I had shared with Matt thirteen years earlier. This was not the first time it had come to mind. From time to time, a glass of red at a dinner party or sipping champagne at a wedding would give me pause to remember that bright spring day. Mostly these thoughts passed as quickly as they had come. But watching *Somm* had been different. The floodgates of wine curiosity had opened wide. Why did wine inspire an enthusiasm that so exceeded its inebriating effects? What secrets lay dormant in wine, waiting to be decoded? And could I, after a lifetime of disinterest, read its language and taste its gifts?

The next day I called Matt. It had been a month since I had last messaged him, congratulating him on Ella's birth. We updated each other on our lives. Matt's newborn baby girl was wonderful, and Luise was in good spirits. As well as navigating his role as a father of three, Matt was in the middle of a massive rebuild at the winery. His vision of a spacious and superbly designed cellar door was being realised. It was a lot of work, but Matt was energised by it. He longed to walk through the finished space.

I was between consulting gigs, soon to start a year-long project for an organisation I loved. As always, I was reading a lot. I had just finished *The Choice* by Dr Edith Eger. It was an astounding memoir by a Holocaust survivor who had become a pre-eminent psychologist later in life. Dr Eger's story of humanity, resilience and insight was remarkable. I enthusiastically suggested to Matt that he read it immediately. Matt agreed that he probably should, but he didn't have a lot of time for reading.

'Fair enough,' I said. 'Also, I watched *Somm* last night. Have you seen it?'

He had, and had enjoyed it. In fact, he knew one of the somms featured. We discussed how insane the process of becoming a Master Sommelier was.

'I've decided I want to learn about wine,' I announced.

'Great! You should check out the courses run by the Wine & Spirit Education Trust. They're really good.'

'No, I want *you* to teach me about wine.'

'Oh, okay,' he said. 'I'm not sure I'm the best person. I mean, I'd be happy to teach you what I know, but I think you'd probably learn more from one of those courses.'

'Well, maybe. But I don't just want to learn about wine. I want to explore the ideas that come with it. It seems to me that wine is loaded with meaning. Do you remember that conversation we had about riesling all those years ago?'

Matt remembered it. He thought of it often. He had

loved Proust's maxim: 'The real voyage of discovery consists not in seeking new landscapes, but in having new eyes.' It had rolled around in his mind over the years. Now and again, he had considered the ways in which wine and winemaking had changed his perception of life itself.

'Well, how about we pick up the conversation again?' I asked.

'It sounds like a great idea. I just don't know when I'll find the time. It's been so hectic.'

'When did you last take some time for yourself?'

He honestly couldn't remember.

'Cool, so you're going to take some time off Wednesday next week,' I commanded. 'This is non-negotiable. I'm going to travel over and you're making yourself available.'

I was surprised by my sudden bossiness, but Matt agreed to the proposal with good humour.

'I'm going to start you off with my favourite: shiraz,' he said. 'Are you good with red wine?'

'Well, I don't hate it.'

'By the time I'm done with you, you'll love it!'

I was curious to see if this prediction would come true.

When I arrived at the winery, Matt gave me a warm hug.

He was excited to show me the progress of the renovations. With sweeping gestures, he guided me through the evolution of the 'cellar door'. Where I saw bare slabs, dust and piles of tools, Matt saw fabulous dining areas with striking decor. Where I saw woodchip, gravel and stones, he saw a lush garden teeming with customers.

Surveying the garden's layout, I was struck by the steady hum of nature. A cacophony of bird and insect music filled the air. An orchestra without a conductor. I was reminded of a book I had read in high school. Written by the pioneering biologist and environmentalist Rachel Carson, *Silent Spring* was published in 1962 as a warning against the use of toxic pesticides. In the opening chapter, Carson describes a fictional town cursed with a 'strange stillness'. The noises of spring had been stifled through the poisoning of the local fauna. Spring was not meant to be quiet. Its natural state is one of vibrating sound. I took it as a sign of health in the place where we stood that this spring was anything but silent.

Matt took me to his upstairs corner office. Large windows looked out onto the cellar door and the surrounding landscape. I was interested to see various items illustrated in Mandarin calligraphy littered about the place. Matt told me they were gifts from Chinese clients. There were also framed, brightly coloured drawings dedicated to 'Daddy' placed lovingly on display. I smiled when I saw them.

I picked up the lone trophy sitting in the office. Having assumed it was an award for winemaking, I was surprised to find it was a prize for saucisson. It turned out that Matt and his cousin had won it for their wild rabbit and pork salami, which they called 'Bastardo'!

Matt laughed when I asked him why this trophy deserved pride of place. He just loved the award. Making salami made him happy.

I put down the trophy. He picked up a bottle from his desk and presented it me.

'Here we go,' he said. 'My shiraz, for our first lesson!'

I examined the bottle. In that moment it held the same significance as a philosophical tome or great work of literature. This was more than an object I could hold in my hand. It was a gateway to understanding. I loved the feeling of being a student again. I was thrilled by the sheer potential of what I might learn. In the words of the Zen master Shunryu Suzuki: 'In the beginner's mind there are many possibilities, but in the expert's there are few.' It was exciting to be a beginner.

'I've got the perfect spot to enjoy this, too,' Matt said. 'I'm taking you to the grand ravine.'

We boarded Matt's mud-spattered SUV and were on our way. I was on 'gate duty', jumping in and out of the car periodically to open gates in accordance with Matt's instructions: 'Left gate in, right gate out.' He played tour guide, pointing out buildings, fields of vines and properties as we went. Soon we were driving through a corridor of gums, their branches and leaves interlacing overhead. The car jostled and jumped along as I held the safety handle above the door, acclimating to our off-roading.

Finally, Matt pulled up. We had arrived. Now we had a walk to take, which included climbing over a *barbed wire fence*. I was unimpressed with this eventuality, but Matt showed me the 'trick' for getting across unharmed. There was a specific point along the fence that could be pushed down without the barbs stabbing into my hand. Once this was done, I could gingerly step over the fence while narrowly avoiding the steel spikes that threatened the integrity of my tan chinos. Once this precarious task was accomplished, Matt assured me that it was 'all downhill' from there. Both literally and figuratively.

The 'grand ravine' was so named for Matt's eldest daughter Lilli. In her younger years, she had been afraid of monsters. Matt knew that simply telling her that these scary creatures didn't exist would likely prove fruitless. As with any strongly held belief, the cold light of reason is rarely enough. Instead, Matt's strategy was to replace the monsters with more kindly characters for her imagination: 'A family of lovely giants lives down here. You can't see them right now, but they're looking out for us and making sure nothing bad happens.' As the mythology of the giants grew, so too did the legend of their home. The 'grand ravine' was the only suitable name for such a phantasmagorical spot.

As we made our way, Matt pointed out that the grand ravine was neither particularly grand nor a ravine. In truth, it was a moderately sized gorge. I didn't mind much either way, as I was already taken in by the surroundings. Granite boulders emerged through the carpet of grass, protruding in clusters of pale pink, red and moss-covered rock. Gum trees and ferns populated the landscape in various stages of growth and decline. The density of bush blunted the wind and provided a cloistered stillness. The most prevalent sound was that of stream water running fresh and clear at the bottom of the gorge. That, and the chirping conversation of orange-breasted finches gossiping among the branches.

This place felt ancient. It *was* ancient. The granite here had been formed some three hundred and seventy million years earlier, when silica-rich magma had struggled its way up through the earth. A 'failed volcano' is what Matt had called it, as the magma had never managed to break the surface. Instead, it had cooled and crystallised a few kilometres underground, an alchemy of feldspar, quartz and mica. Over time, erosion had exposed the igneous rock treasured beneath.

Aside from the occasional saw-cut tree stump, there was almost no sign of human activity. It was easy to imagine we had been lost in time – transported hundreds of years into the past or future. There was no phone reception either, compounding the sense of remoteness. I was eager not to stumble into a *Picnic at Hanging Rock* scenario, spirited away without hope of return. If this was *Picnic at Hanging Rock*, I would most likely have landed the role of the stout girl fated to run from the scene, screaming 'Miiiiraaanda!'

As we made our descent, Matt moved with the confidence of a highwire acrobat, stepping with sure-footed precision. I fumbled my way down. I felt adolescently clumsy and wholly over-dressed. Maybe my blue Alexander McQueen cardigan wasn't the right choice after all? The fear of falling and spoiling my knitwear was profound.

We reached our spot, which turned out to be a hefty boulder immersed in ferns. Matt made his way to the top of the boulder in three quick moves. After some serious manoeuvring, and narrowly avoiding a fall, I joined him.

The view was gorgeous. Matt remarked that it looked like an Arthur Streeton painting. From our position the stream was clearly visible, meandering through the lowest part of the gorge. The vegetation on either side of the water was brightly nourished. One tree in particular reminded me of a Japanese woodblock print, its branches stretched above the stream in a semi-cascade, like a bonsai. We were both silent for a moment, taking in the sights and smells of eucalyptus, bracken and earth.

I shuffled on the boulder so Matt could get to the pack on my back. He extracted two plastic wine glasses and the bottle of shiraz. He deftly filled the glasses without spilling a drop. He handed me one of them and returned the bottle to the backpack.

'So, shiraz is the wine we are best known for,' Matt began, jumping straight into the lesson. 'It has a robust character but is also capable of nuance. If you were going to describe it as a person, it would be a tall, dark and handsome Renaissance man.'

I was liking the sound of shiraz already!

'Now, in wine-tasting we assess the qualities of the wine through sight, smell and taste,' Matt continued. 'We start by looking at the wine and considering its colour. How would you describe the colour of this shiraz?'

I held my glass up to eye level.

'Um, it's red?'

Matt looked at me and laughed. 'We have a long way to go, don't we?'

I laughed too.

'So, I would say it's a deep dark red, with some youthful purple,' he said.

I looked at the wine. 'Sure,' I thought. 'Purple.'

'Okay, now to smell.'

Matt swirled the wine in his glass. He put his nose close to the rim and took a deep breath. I copied.

'Do you notice any one smell that jumps out at you?' he asked. 'Does it remind you of something? You can say "red wine", that's fine.'

Determined to impress my friend, I took a moment to consider. 'Okay, I'd say I'm smelling some flowers.'

He smiled. 'Spot on. This shiraz is a very aromatic style, and we often describe it as having aromas of violets.'

I tried again. It was like a blossom-filled garden on a cold, wet day – raindrops clinging to the edge of purple and blue petals before falling to the lawn below.

The final step was taste. At first, I was tempted to say that it tasted like 'red wine', but I persevered. I took a couple more sips. On the last sip I tasted plum.

Matt nodded with approval. 'Yeah, that's right where I'd put it as well, in that darker fruit territory – blackberries or bramble berries or, like you say, plums.'

Vladimir Nabokov, the famed author of the infamous novel *Lolita*, wrote in his 1951 memoir *Speak, Memory* about a condition called synaesthesia. This peculiar affliction causes the 'synaesthete' to experience their senses as 'mixed together'. This might mean hearing smells, tasting shapes, seeing flavours or feeling sounds. In Nabokov's case, he experienced 'grapheme-colour' synaesthesia, in which he saw letters of the alphabet in specific colours. For him, 'V' was a pale pink and 'C' was a light blue. I was reminded of this muddling as I considered the presence of 'plum' in my glass. It was strange how this purple-tinted liquid might evoke the smell of a purple flower and the taste of a purple fruit. This shiraz was 'purple' in more ways than one. It almost felt like I was drinking colour. Maybe wine appreciation would unlock a synaesthetic part of my brain?

'This is really nice,' I said, complimenting Matt on his creation. 'I could see shiraz becoming a favourite.'

'You know,' said Matt, 'one of the great things about shiraz is that it can be grown in a broad range of climates and made in a variety of styles. So, you can have shiraz grown in warmer climates which is typically bigger, riper and more muscular. A riper style generally has more fruit sweetness, structure and alcohol. It's bold, powerful and immediately impressive. Some excellent examples come from regions like the Barossa Valley or McLaren Vale.'

Shiraz was quite the polymath.

'Then, at our end of the spectrum, you tend to get more restraint and elegance. This comes from grapes grown in a cooler climate. With this style of shiraz, you see less of that apparent sweetness from fruit and alcohol – it tends to be very aromatic and feminine.'

I imagined a woman dressed in a prim Chanel suit, smelling of Schiaparelli's *Shocking* perfume.

'The best examples in the world come from the Rhône Valley in France and the cooler regions in Australia, like the Strathbogies,' Matt said, pointing to an imaginary map of the world. 'These are typically spicier examples with the aroma of white pepper and violets. Think elegance, lifted aromatics, fine mouthfeel, persistent flavour, balance and length. This type of shiraz has layered complexity and is great with food.'

Matt's love for wine was clear. He could produce these

tutorials without a second's thought. It was testament to experience paired with passion.

As he explained shiraz's many talents, I took in more and more of the wine's aroma. I was in love with the floral bouquet.

'To be honest, I think I enjoy the smell more than the taste,' I said, slightly concerned this might be an offensive remark.

'Me too,' beamed Matt, to my relief. 'But I'll get you to do something I learnt from Heston Blumenthal tasting chocolate. Taste it without smelling.'

Feeling like I was playing a primary-school game, I held my nostrils shut with my left thumb and index finger. I took a sip.

'Okay, that tastes really boring,' I said.

'Now, do it again but let go of your nose half-way through the sip this time.'

As I released my nostrils mid-sip, a wonderful richness was unleashed on my palate. It was like in *The Wizard of Oz*, when Dorothy transitions from the sepia stains of Kansas to the technicolour bonanza of Oz.

'Right, so you definitely need smell,' I said.

'Yeah, it's a massive part of the overall experience of wine. We put a lot of time into aroma. It's just so important.'

I was still wearing my backpack, and shuffled around again to give Matt access. I asked him to pull out the book of poems I had brought with me.

'So, when you mentioned we were going to start with shiraz, I had a brainwave,' I began. 'I remembered that Shiraz was the city where the poet Hafiz lived back in the fourteenth century. As it happens, Hafiz wrote poems in which he used wine as a metaphor to express his ideas about Sufism.'

Sufism is the mystical tradition of Islam. Renowned for its spirit of tolerance and inclusivity, it favours a path of self-transcendence and direct experience. The most famous of the Sufi practices is the spiralling dance of the 'whirling dervish' (a dervish being a Sufi initiate). Garbed in voluminous skirts and conical felt hats, the dervishes move round and round like so many spinning tops, with the palm of their right hand facing heaven and the palm of their left hand facing the earth. Receiving and giving, giving and receiving. The music plays ever faster, building to a frenzy of turning and tempo. In the dizzying eddies of their meditation, the dervishes are lost in an ocean of love.

The founding father of the whirling dervishes was the 13th-century Sufi mystic and master poet Jalaluddin Muhammad Balkhi Rumi, or 'Rumi' for short. Following in Rumi's footsteps was Hafiz of Shiraz. Said to have memorised all of Rumi's poetry by heart, Hafiz remains the most popular poet in modern-day Iran.

'Wine seems to have played a major role in Hafiz's spiritual life,' I explained. 'The story goes that to achieve direct experience of the divine, Hafiz sat in a circle for forty days without food or water. On the fortieth day, the Angel Gabriel came to him and released him from the circle. Hafiz rushed to the house of his teacher, who immediately gave him a cup of wine. When he drank the wine, Hafiz finally achieved the spiritual awakening he had been seeking.'

Leafing through the earmarked and underlined sections of my book, I read aloud stanzas of Hafiz's poetry. Images of wine appeared again and again:

'"A brimming cup of wine I prize the most – this is enough for me!"'

'"With wine, with red wine your prayer carpet dye!"'

'"Oh Cup-bearer, set my glass afire with the light of wine!"'

Turning to my friend, I was curious to see what he made of these verses. What reflections did the winemaker have about these seven-hundred-year-old, wine-soaked poems?

'Do you think he was an alcoholic?' he asked.

I started laughing. Matt quickly joined in. It was the most wonderfully unanticipated question. I doubted any serious research had ever gone into the matter, but was there a chance that Hafiz had been in need of a twelve-step program?

'No, I wouldn't think so,' I replied. 'Wine is mostly used as an analogy for love and truth in his poems. Hafiz is all about letting go of our fixation on seeing things in absolutes – black and white, good and evil. For him, wine is all about abandoning the shackles of the everyday and revelling in the beauty of life. It's all about authenticity and appreciation.'

The word 'appreciation' lingered in the air.

'That's what I love about living and working with nature,' Matt said. 'I love being able to share moments with my girls, like smelling a rose or watching a ladybird on a leaf. I love being able to go to the veggie patch and pick a tomato and just connect with the natural world. You take the time to celebrate and honour that tomato because there's no guarantee you're going to get it. Mother Nature gives and Mother Nature takes away. So, you just have to appreciate the little things.'

I heartily agreed. 'What you're describing is a practice of profound appreciation,' I said. 'It's so foreign to us nowadays. We live in this crazy-fast consumer culture that's all about what's next. We consume, we dispose and we consume again. There's no space to enjoy what's right in front of you. It makes me think of poetry. You can read a poem as a short piece of writing and just race through it. But to really get the most out of a poem, you need to spend time with it. You have to sit with it, contemplate it and let the words marinate. It's something of a lost art form.'

Matt held his glass up to the light again.

'You have to take time,' he said. 'That's one of the things you realise when producing fine wine. You start looking for the finest example of everything, whether it's the finest ladybug, the finest flower or the finest produce in the garden. But you have to really slow down to notice the finer things.'

Wondering aloud whether there was a kind of paradox in that, I put the question to Matt: 'Are the finer wines the ones that actually give you greater access to the beauty of the ordinary? Are they the ones that help you best appreciate the smell of a flower or the taste of a berry?'

'Yeah, I think that's right,' Matt responded, boosted by the thought. 'It's the great wine paradox! The finer the wine, the more it draws out your appreciation for everyday things. But the thing about wine, even fine wine, is that it is very ordinary. It comes from an aggressively growing vine that produces fruit that happens to have tartaric acid in it which, in turn, helps us preserve wine. In that sense, it's fairly unremarkable – it's just what nature does. But in the industry, we have a tendency to build all this reverential nonsense and snobbery around it.'

'You know,' I said, 'Hafiz couldn't stand elitism either. In his poems he mocked the hypocrisy of religious puritanism. I suppose wine snobs are the puritans of the wine world. Anyway, Hafiz was all about enjoying life with the commonfolk. I think you and he would have got along.'

Matt laughed. 'I'm sure we would have! I certainly feel all the affectation that comes with wine is over the top. It takes away from the fact that wine is this amazing reflection of nature. Like you say, wine is all about the beauty of the ordinary.'

I was reminded of the 17th-century Dutch painter Johannes Vermeer. He took painstaking time to complete his artworks. He also used an exquisitely expensive palette of colours, including ultramarine made from finely ground lapis lazuli. Despite his love for the finest of paints, his subject matter tended to be more commonplace. Whether it was a kitchen maid pouring a jug of milk, a woman writing a letter or a lacemaker hard at work, Vermeer's paintings celebrated the quiet, inconspicuous moments of everyday life. His remarkable skill as an artist illuminated the value of what is all too easily overlooked.

'It really gives a different meaning to the term "wine appreciation",' I said. 'There's wine appreciation where you learn to appreciate the wine. But there's also wine appreciation where you learn to appreciate life.'

Matt beamed. 'I love that! You know, I would have had a thousand different thoughts about these things over the years, but never articulated them. Talking with you now, I can see things more clearly. With the winery and the kids, I'm just so busy. But it feels good to take the time.'

This time I thought of Socrates. 'A wise man once said "the unexamined life is not worth living". Maybe that's a bit extreme, but the point remains. I think it's important to pause and reflect, and what better way to do it than over a glass of wine and a beautiful view?'

It really was such a beautiful view. It was strange to think that we were only an hour and a half's drive out of Melbourne. The landscape of life was so different here – older and quieter. The apparent order of city life gave way to another sense of order, one less obvious but more enduring. As much as Melbourne was my home, I could see the wisdom of Matt's refuge among the granite and the trees.

'Let's do this again soon,' said Matt.

'I would love to,' I replied.

CHAPTER 3
Pinot Noir

'My question to you is, what do we do first?'

'We check the colour of the wine. I'll try not to just say "red".'

Two months had passed since my last meeting with Matt and the weather had warmed. My knitwear had been archived for another year. I dreaded the coming of the Australian summer. While friends relished shining days with feet in the sand and shirts tossed aside, I shied away to air-conditioned comfort. I aimed to avoid the stickiness of the season. I associated summer with sweat-stained clothes clinging to every trouble spot. In the peak months, the world became a convection oven. I couldn't see the appeal.

On this summer's day, the temperature was mercifully mild at the vineyard. Matt had suggested that we enjoy our wine by the dam. When the skies were clear, the water was azure. Bordered by fields of vines and distant gums, it was a more picturesque location than the word 'dam' suggested. Also, the vines nearby were the same that produced the wine we would be drinking – pinot noir.

As we drove to our watering hole, Matt explained that the

vineyard was in 'flowering and fruit set'. It was a decisive moment in the growth of the grape. As the heat comes, the vines flourish with clusters of tiny flowers. These flowers pollinate themselves and transform into the grape berries. It is a treacherous time, when too much wind or rain can harm the formation of the flowers. If the flowers do not develop, the grapes will not come. A successful flowering and fruit set is the foundation of a prosperous vintage.

We pulled over and dismounted from the SUV. I was glad I had applied SPF 50+ sunscreen beforehand. My Anglo-Saxon skin did not fare well under the ultraviolet light of the Australian sun. More than the risk of skin cancer, vanity made me vigilant in the use of sunblock lotions. When I saw friends with sunburnt faces, I would never mention melanomas. Instead, I would chastise them about the 'signs of ageing': 'Do you want to turn into a leather handbag? Do you want to look like Donatella Versace?'

I followed Matt to our drinking spot by the water. We sat on the lately mown dry grass. A charming breeze rippled over the dam, refreshing the air. The chirping of crickets mingled with the soft calls of sheep carried on the wind. Matt produced two glasses and a bottle of pinot noir from his brown leather satchel. He opened the bottle with practised efficiency. My eyes wandered across the horizon. The sky was almost entirely clear, except for a scattering of small cumulus clouds floating like faraway balls of cotton wool. Apart from these fluffy blotches of white, the sky was a vast ceiling of blue.

'Here we go, mate,' Matt said, handing me a glass. 'Let's get the next lesson underway.'

He talked me through the tasting process again – sight, smell and taste. Unlike older pinot noirs, which might be 'brick red' or 'garnet', this pinot was a bright cherry red. The wine smelt of Morello cherries, raspberries, cranberries and strawberries. Other types of pinot might have more earthy aromas, reminiscent of barnyard, bracken and forest floor. As for flavour, it was cherries again. Juicy red cherries.

'Pinot is naturally high in acid,' Matt explained. 'It really gets your mouth watering. Like riesling, the high acid means pinot goes well with a wide variety of foods.'

Matt's winery was interested in crafting wine to specifically match wild game meat. An avid hunter from his childhood days, Matt held that game meat was a socially conscious and sustainable alternative to factory farming. Creating wines to pair with wild food was a natural step. If you needed a chardonnay to match with rabbit or a shiraz to pair with venison, he had you covered. For Matt, food and wine were intertwined like the double-helix strands of a DNA molecule.

'Which foods would you pair with this pinot?' I asked.

'Anything that has some fat would be good because the acid would help cut through it. For example, a fatty salami would be an excellent match. The wine would support the taste of the salami by mopping up some of the fat. It cleanses the palate. Likewise, the fat would calm down the sense of acid in the wine.'

'If you were going to serve a meal to complement this wine, what would you make?'

'This pinot would be fantastic matched with a wild boar ragout tossed through pappardelle and roasted chestnuts. It would go great with a chicken and leek pie made with smoky bacon. Pinot noir goes really well with bacon. You could also have it with a charcuterie platter of salami, prosciutto, capocollo and a quality aged cheddar. For a simpler option, a last-of-season basil pesto scraped over dense, slightly-over-toasted sourdough would be perfect.'

I was suddenly hungry. Why hadn't we packed a picnic?

'This is the least formal pinot we make,' Matt remarked. 'In truth, it's the pinot I reach for most, which probably says something about me!'

Even as a novice, I could see why. This wine struck me as light on the palate. 'It feels easy to drink. I would say it's a wine you'd enjoy when you want to just kick back. Maybe that's what it says about you; that you need to take the pressure down.'

'Lu and the kids would definitely agree with you at the moment.'

Turning to the rows of vines in view, I asked how the year's crop of pinot noir was faring.

'It's going well so far, but it's early days,' Matt replied. 'Pinot's so hit and miss.'

'Why?'

'Growing pinot noir grapes is a real art form. You can't push them around. They have very thin skin, which makes them susceptible to all kinds of problems. If Mother Nature gives you a hard time, the grape will just go to pieces.'

'As a wine grower, that must be pretty stressful.'

'Definitely. In fact, they call it the "heartbreak grape" for that very reason. It's normal for pinot vintages to fail every now and then, depending on the region they're grown in.'

The heartbreak grape. In considering a bottle of wine, it was easy to forget the human cost. Failed vintages meant failed livelihoods. So much hard work lost to the vagaries of weather or disease. As thin as the pinot grape's skin was, the wine grower's skin had to be twice as thick.

'Not only is growing pinot noir challenging,' Matt continued, 'but the winemaking process is also extremely delicate. You have to get just the right balance between fruit and tannin. It's hard to grow and hard to make, which is one of the reasons it's more expensive than other varieties.'

'Why bother with pinot at all? It sounds like a hassle.'

'Because if you make it through and get it right, pinot is mercurial. One of the most exciting wines I've ever had was a pinot noir. In the wine industry, we would say it has the "peacock's tail". It encompasses the full spectrum of aromas and flavours in a way I can't really describe. If wine was quantified in percentages, this one would be one hundred per cent. To me, there is nothing missing. It's complete.'

I enjoyed the metaphor of the peacock's tail. The iridescent blue, turquoise and green feathers pluming from the male peafowl represented divinity in mythologies around the world. The peacock is associated with the blue-skinned Hindu god Krishna; the compassionate Buddhist goddess Guan Yin; and Hera, the Queen of the ancient Greek gods. The pinot noir that Matt described sounded like a beverage fit for a heavenly being.

'In short,' I said, 'pinot noir is remarkably fragile but worth all the problems because of how good the wine can be.'

'Pretty much.'

'You know, the way you describe pinot reminds me of a troubled, creative genius. A sensitive soul who feels things deeply and sees things differently. Someone who's tortured and unstable but can also make masterpieces if the world doesn't crush them first.'

I was thinking of Virginia Woolf. The author of such lyrically groundbreaking books as *Mrs Dalloway* and *The Waves*, she also wrestled with bouts of depression and mania. Nowadays, she would likely be diagnosed with bipolar disorder. Her husband Leonard supported her in every way he could. Unfortunately, Virginia lived in a time before effective treatments for her condition were available. She ended her life in 1941 by walking into the River Ouse in southern England.

'A sensitive soul – that's pinot in a nutshell,' Matt said. 'It's a gentle little grape that's capable of so much but often finds life too hard. One of the things we did to support our pinot was to massively reduce our yields. We went down to one bunch per cane, which is extraordinarily light.'

The cane, I discovered, is the woody part of the vine that carries the leaves and bunches of grapes.

'Reducing the yield wasn't a great commercial decision,' Matt explained. 'Where we would normally get three tonnes of pinot grapes to the acre, we were only producing half a tonne. The thing is, it's not about turning profit. It's about passion. We took the pressure off the pinot to see what we could unlock. It worked. We learnt to make pinot by being accommodating and looking after it.'

I turned to my friend and smiled. 'It's sort of fitting that you enjoy this pinot when you need to calm down. After all the work you put into looking after the grape, it looks after you in return.'

Matt nodded. 'I've never thought of a wine as looking after me, but I suppose that's true. My wines look after me in a lot of different ways.'

I decided then and there that we're all a bit like pinot noir. 'Human beings are sensitive, and need support. The problem is that so many of us don't value sensitivity, and we're often ashamed to ask for help. We tend to see it as a weakness. We forget that sensitivity is a source of expression and artistry, consideration and empathy. We also forget that asking for help is such an important way for us to connect with other people.'

The last time I had visited Matt's home I had spotted a book on social anxiety in the study. I instinctively knew it was his. My friend, who travelled the world to sell his wines and commanded a sprawling business, had also purchased a book on shyness. Human beings can be such contradictory creatures – at once obvious and unfathomable. The way we are and the way we are seen is so often at odds. Like a dark reservoir of water concealed beneath layers of rock, our stalwart exteriors belie a hidden gentleness.

'Not only do we devalue sensitivity,' I said, 'we pathologise it. People are taught that if they're not coping then there must be something wrong with them. Most of the time we don't look at the pressures that others might be dealing with and ask: "Are we expecting too much?" Sometimes people simply can't cope with the amount of strain they're under. What's more, we shouldn't expect them to. I think pinot's a great example of that.'

'Exactly!' Matt enthused. 'You can't just say to pinot: "You've got to suck it up." If you're getting lots of rain or excessive heat, it won't happen. You have to adjust the environment around it. Pinot's quite happy to grow if you support and nurture it. I think you're absolutely right that the same is true with people. I've seen so many friends suffer …'

He trailed off. From time to time, Matt posted on social media about the mental health of farmers. Compared to the general Australian male population, male farmers are twice as likely to commit suicide. News articles described the factors at play – drought, economic hardship, loneliness. The stereotypical stoicism of the rural Australian male was also held to account. The bush-hardened Aussie bloke is not known for his effusiveness, and it's difficult to help those who struggle to show their suffering.

'If you were to think of your stereotypical Australian male farmer,' Matt said, 'the words "nurturing" or "gentle" probably wouldn't spring to mind. But I can tell you first-hand that some of the kindest men I know are farmers. These are men who seem as tough as nails but who will get up before daybreak to make sure their baby lambs are okay.'

'That's very sweet,' I said, touched by the thought of these weather-hardened blokes checking on their flock of lambs in the wee hours.

'If you were to ask any of them,' Matt continued, 'they'd probably shrug it off by saying they're looking after their investment. But nobody cares that much about money to check on their baby lambs at three am. There is kindness and softness in everyone. It's just not always obvious.'

'I can't imagine what it's like living off the land,' I said.

'We talk about adjusting the environment around people to better support them. But that's difficult to do when your circumstances are determined by nature itself.'

Matt nodded in agreement. 'I don't think I ever told you the full story of what happened when I started the winery. As you know, I was full of enthusiasm to make a life in the bush. But pretty much as soon I started, Mother Nature absolutely kicked the shit out of me. It was four years before I got a break. I thought I was going to lose everything.'

I shook my head. 'I remember speaking to you a couple of times about things being difficult, but you always put an optimistic spin on it.'

'I remember standing right here with Lu, looking down at an empty dam with fires raging fifty kilometres away. I'd be lying if I said there wasn't a tear rolling down my cheek. I said to Lu: "Sorry, babe, I think I've fucked it."'

I had no idea it had got that bad. The beginning of Matt's winemaking journey foreshadowed the coming four years. The winery's former owners had become insolvent. This had sent shock waves through the local community, leaving many families in financial hardship. The insolvency created numerous hurdles that delayed the purchase of the property. By the time Matt took possession, it was late in the vintage. The harvest was rushed and uncomfortable.

The vintage after that proved even more challenging. When summer came, fires raged in the high country, blanketing the landscape in acrid smoke. For thirty days the fires burnt, sooty air contaminating the vine leaves, grapes and soil.

'The smell of smoke permeated everything,' Matt said, with a look of disgust. 'It was in every corner of the house. It was in all our clothes. You couldn't escape it.'

I shuddered at the thought of my treasured items of apparel drenched in the odour of bushfire.

'It was also a steep learning curve,' he said. 'The science of how to manage vines and grapes with that level of smoke damage is unclear. There wasn't much research because it wasn't a common problem in the past. It's becoming a much bigger issue with climate change. We did our best, but the wine turned out pretty ordinary.'

Instead of bushfires, the next vintage was blighted by a heatwave. Day after day, temperatures topping 40 degrees Celsius caused all the vines to ripen at once. The winemaking calendar was thrown topsy-turvy. It was impossible for the winery to process the amount of ripe fruit they had on their hands. Matt hired refrigerated trucks to store the grapes and manage the temperature of the ferments.

'That heatwave wiped out so many vintages,' he recalled. 'It was hard because everyone was already struggling with the drought.'

Starting in 2001, the so-called 'Millennium Drought' devastated agriculture in the south-east of Australia for nine consecutive years. The autumn rains grew scarce. Green fields turned yellow and dusty. Dams ran dry, crops failed and farm animals perished. It was one of the worst droughts in Australia's recorded history.

'Then there were all the commercial difficulties,' Matt continued. 'It was such an extreme time for winemaking in Australia.'

On top of that, in 2007, the global financial crisis hit. Although many Australian industries were shielded from the full impact of the economic disaster, the wine industry was not. High exchange rates, retailer consolidation and structural oversupply all culminated in a monumental market crash. There were too many bottles and not enough buyers.

'I had parcels of wine I couldn't liquidate at *any* price, irrespective of the quality,' Matt said. 'Such a shame. It was good wine.'

This run of bad fortune reached its nadir in the summer of 2009, when about four hundred bushfires ravaged the Victorian countryside. Known collectively as the Black Saturday fires, they destroyed more than two thousand homes and took 173 lives. It was a national tragedy. As a volunteer with the Country Fire Authority, Matt witnessed the immediate aftermath first-hand.

'I'll never forget what I saw that day after the fires had torn through,' he said. 'We went in to mop up and it was like a moonscape. There was ash and powder everywhere. It reminded me of an antique photo. Everything was grey.

We came round the corner of this totally decimated house and there were kids' clothes hanging on the clothesline. They hadn't been burnt. It was the eeriest, weirdest thing I've ever seen. These brightly coloured children's clothes against a backdrop of ashen grey. I remember feeling sick. To this day, I don't know if that family made it out alive.'

Surrounded by such terrible loss of life, Matt felt blessed that the fires never reached the vineyard. But the smoke did. The skies turned red and the countryside was veiled in a dirty mist. Once again, the vines and grapes were swamped in polluted air.

'It was another year of tiny, dehydrated berries,' Matt said. 'That, combined with the financial difficulties and all the destruction around us, meant everything seemed fairly hopeless.'

I realised that as Matt had been talking, I had been absent-mindedly pulling at the grass beside me. I stopped, leaving a small pile of broken grass blades and uprooted soil. I looked across again at the field of vines. The way that the rows formed lines in the landscape reminded me of the patterned rake marks in a Zen garden. On such a bright and gentle day, it was difficult to comprehend nature's violence and chaos.

'After all that, how did you *not* throw in the towel?' I asked.

'I don't know,' he said, tilting his head as he considered the question. 'What is resilience? How does it work? I just felt like I had to stay and fight. Thank goodness I did, because in 2010, Mother Nature turned everything around. The drought broke and the weather was beautiful. We had a classic cool vintage with temperatures only as high as thirty degrees and blue skies every day. It was the best vintage in the history of the Strathbogie Ranges.'

'What a relief after four years of hell!'

'It wasn't all bad, not by a long shot. In some ways, it was a really happy time in our lives. We were pushing new frontiers, connecting with the farm, and getting to know everyone. We were also doing lots of lovely day-to-day stuff like learning to grow vegetables. Simple things.'

Matt took a hearty gulp of wine.

'I also grew a lot in the process,' he said. 'I had quite a structured, disciplined upbringing at school. It was a huge awakening for me, learning to live with uncertainty.'

'How do you avoid getting overwhelmed by it?'

'It's a tough one. You can't be rigid. You just have to follow your gut and work with whatever comes your way. Once you've done that, you reassess and make different choices. You do that over and over again. It never ends. You're always changing and evolving in response to the whims of the environment.'

Out on the dam, gentle patterns came and went as the air moved over the surface of the water.

'Be like water,' I murmured.

Matt shot me a quizzical glance. 'What do you mean?'

'A key concept in the ancient Chinese philosophy of Taoism is "wu wei", which roughly translates as "non-action" or "action without effort". It's a bit of a misleading term because it's not about sitting around doing nothing. Wu wei describes an approach for acting in harmony with nature. The Taoists use the image of water to illustrate the point. They say the strongest element is not earth or fire, but water. Although water appears gentle, it can wear away the hard and unmoving rock. Its strength lies in its ability to flow.'

I pointed to the horizon, where the supple branches of gum trees swayed against the sky.

'The Taoist philosopher Zhuangzi used the metaphor of the willow tree. If the branches of a tree are stiff and brittle, they will break in a strong wind. The branches of the willow tree will remain intact because they move *with* the wind, not against it. It's a paradox. True power isn't found in being hard and inflexible. It's found in changing and adapting to whatever is happening in the moment.'

'That's exactly right,' Matt said. 'If you're rigid with Mother Nature, it doesn't work. You have to be sensitive to her moods and work with them.'

I took a sip. The taste of cherries washed over my tongue. I considered the contents of my almost empty glass.

'Funnily enough,' I said, 'Zhuangzi also explained wu wei by describing a drunken man falling out of a carriage. The drunkard doesn't hurt himself because he doesn't resist the fall. He doesn't tense up when he hits the ground and, because of that, he walks away unharmed.'

Matt laughed. 'Who said that drinking isn't good for you?'

A phone rang. As the ringtone wasn't Blondie singing 'Call Me', I knew it was Matt's phone. He promptly answered the call. It was a quick conversation, over in a couple of minutes.

He hung up. 'One moment I'm talking about Chinese philosophy, the next about pest control. Sorry mate, we should probably make a move. Lots to do.'

'Absolutely,' I replied. 'Let's head back. You're a busy man!'

While we wiped the grass from our backsides, a magpie landed nearby. Its head turned sharply and inquisitively. It squawked three times and flew away. It came and went so quickly; it was easy to wonder whether it was ever there at all.

As always, I struggled to climb aboard the SUV. So much effort was required between standing on the ground and assuming a seated position. Farm life struck me as uncomfortably labour-intensive. Like with summer, I was at a loss to see the appeal.

While we drove, we discussed our plans for the coming week. Matt updated me on the cellar door building project. It was proving slower and more expensive than he would have liked, but that was par for the course. As we spoke, I stared out the passenger-seat window.

'Did you know that the sky isn't actually blue?' I asked.

Matt turned to me, surprised by the abrupt change of topic. He let out a warm laugh. 'Where do you come up with this stuff?'

I smiled. 'I was reading an article about it. It explained that the sky is transparent and has no colour at all. The sky *appears* to be coloured because of how different wavelengths from the sun's light are scattered in the atmosphere. Because blue and violet wavelengths are shorter, they are scattered the most.'

'Then why isn't the sky violet?'

'Good question. All things being equal, the sky should be a bluish-violet colour. But because of the way our eyes filter and perceive colour, we see the sky as light blue.'

'That's super weird to think about.'

I gazed at the horizon. Try as I might to see the sky differently, its colour remained the same. I couldn't detect the faintest shade of violet. The sky was stubbornly, resolutely, swear-on-a-stack-of-bibles blue.

'I suppose it's a good reminder,' I said quietly. 'If you ever need proof that things aren't always as they seem, just go outside on a clear day and look up.'

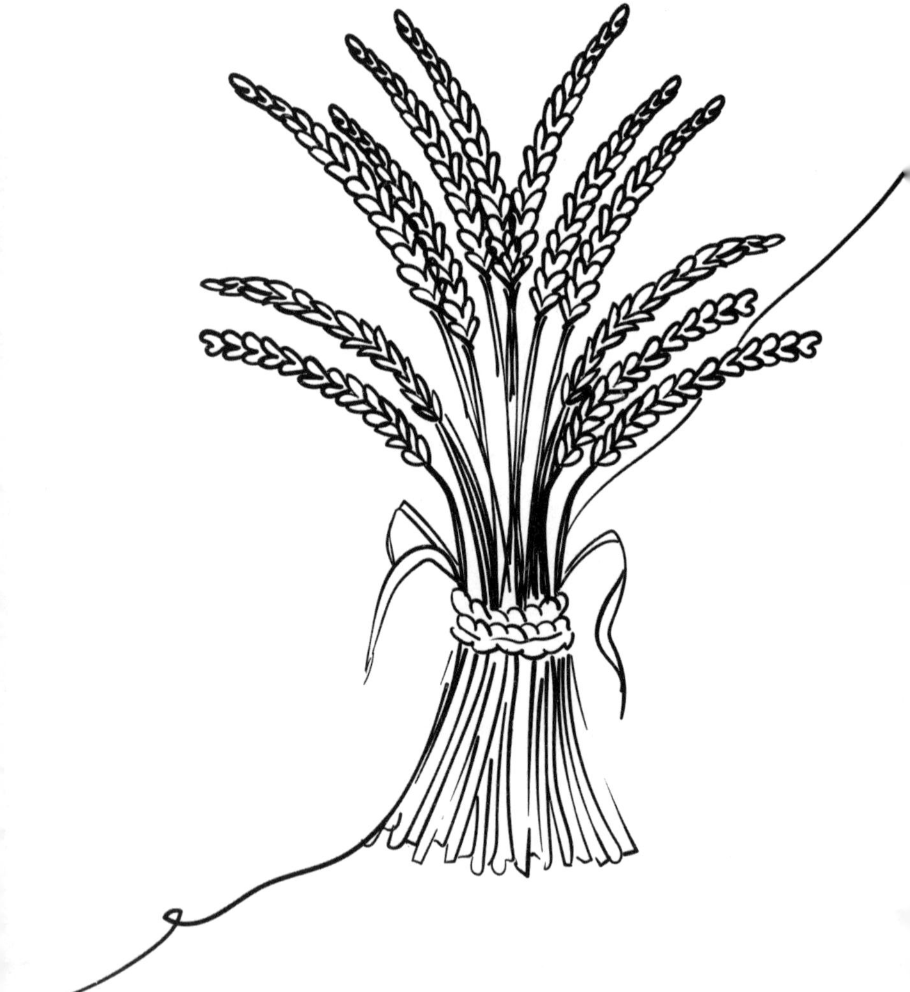

CHAPTER 4
Chardonnay

'What can a person do when he thinks of all the things he cannot understand, but look at the fields of wheat?'

Vincent van Gogh wrote this while living in Arles in southern France. It is safe to assume that the artist spent considerable time pondering things he could not understand. It was in Arles that he created some of his most stunning interpretations of the landscape, among them the *Harvest* pictures. This series of ten paintings and five drawings portrays scenes from the wheatfields of Provence. They were produced in just over a week, the artist working tirelessly under the blazing sun. The only reason he stopped the series was because a storm brought the harvest to a sudden close. This was in June of 1888, two years before his death.

For Van Gogh, the harvest had sublime significance. He saw something divine in the toil of the peasants reaping and gathering. Birth and death, creation and destruction, struggle and salvation. It was all there. As if to portray this spiritual wealth, he painted wheat glowing like gold. Stacks of hay could be mistaken for piles of treasure. Where others might see an unremarkable moment in rural life, Van Gogh saw a world alive with emotion and meaning. Not only did he see this world, he was also able to share it with others. It was his rare gift to alchemise the mundane into the miraculous with a paint stroke.

'How would you describe this colour?' Matt asked, holding his glass aloft.

'It's quite beautiful. It reminds me of Van Gogh's *Harvest* paintings. A gorgeous shade of gold.'

We were drinking chardonnay, standing in the middle of Matt's vineyard, with bunches of burgeoning shiraz grapes all around us. It was absurdly idyllic. I felt like we were posing for a lifestyle blog. Wasn't this something I had seen members of the Dutch royal family do in *Hello!* magazine?

'This one smells of apple blossom,' Matt said. 'But there's also a buttery aroma. Can you smell buttered popcorn?'

'I was wondering why I had the image of a cinema concession stand in my head! Yes, buttered popcorn and something else … pineapple?'

Matt agreed. Blossom, butter and tropical fruit, all in one glass. It was quite the combination.

'I'm getting crisp apple,' I said after the first sip.

'Definitely,' Matt replied. 'I can taste apple and citrus fruits. I can taste a lot of things. The thing with this wine is its complexity. It's hard to define one main characteristic. They all meld together. It's soft yet firm, light yet grippy. It's the full spectrum.'

'The peacock's tail?'

'You could say that! You've got all these elements dancing on your tongue at once. Many of these characters stay with you long after you've finished. This wine also has what we call "length".'

Taking another sip, I waited to see what happened. He was right. Flavours lingered in the most pleasing way. It was like the afterglow of a freshly extinguished light, leaving a warm halo hanging in the air.

'It's not a hard and fast rule,' Matt said, 'but higher quality wines generally have greater length.'

I could see the parallels in everyday life. 'It's usually a sign of quality when something's built to last,' I noted. 'Of course, I imagine there are cases in which length isn't a good thing. For example, when you drink a crappy wine and you can't get the bad taste out of your mouth and you have to pop a Mentos.'

He laughed. 'Good point.'

We were walking as we talked. Matt had brought me to the vineyard to show me 'veraison'. This is the time when the grapes begin to ripen, swelling in size and sweetness as carbohydrates from the roots and trunk flow to the fruit. Prior to veraison, an untrained eye would have little hope in telling red from white. All unripe grapes are green. Once the grapes ripen, they transform into the colour of their variety. Cabernet grapes purple and darken, while riesling grapes turn a ruddy yellow. Veraison is the grape's adolescence.

'I love how the grapes look,' I remarked, pointing to a particularly large bunch. 'The combination of different coloured berries makes me think of an ancient Roman mosaic.'

It was clear, even to me, that the mosaic effect was due to the individual grapes ripening at different rates. As with any group of teenagers, some matured quickly while others took their time. The late bloomers would inevitably catch up, but before then each bunch was a many-hued family. Some grapes were green, others reddish-purple and some a marbled mixture of green-reddish-purple. There didn't seem to be any uniformity as to which grapes ripened first. A cluster of dark, sugar-flushed grapes might encircle a solitary baby green grape, and vice versa. Each grape had its own path, unrelated to the progress of its siblings.

'Chardonnay is a strong variety when it comes to both diversity and complexity,' Matt said, leading me back to the matter at hand. 'It takes to winemaking well. It's a canvas you can paint in a million different ways. You can have a crisp and fresh chardonnay, like those traditionally made in the Chablis region in France. Or you can have a buttery, wooded chardonnay, like the ones they make in California. The possibilities are endless, which is why many call chardonnay the "queen of the whites".'

I figured that this meant chardonnay was the most popular variety of white wine, but Matt explained that this wasn't necessarily so.

'Its popularity has changed over time,' he told me. 'Wines go in and out of fashion. Back in the seventies, a sweeter style of riesling was dominant, but that quickly waned. Then chardonnay became the dominant force. After that, sauvignon blanc rose to prominence. As you'll learn, sauvignon blanc is an immediately exciting variety. It's up-front and unashamed, which makes it easy to enjoy. Nowadays, chardonnay's back in style. But no matter which white is popular at the time, chardonnay always keeps trucking along in the background.'

'It sounds like chardonnay is the Chanel suit of white wine,' I mused. 'Other styles come and go, but the classics never die.'

'Absolutely. Chardonnay will travel with you on your wine journey and never lose relevance. Not once. It's an amazing variety.'

I realised I had been drinking a little faster than usual. The wine was lovely and chilled. A perfect balm for the afternoon heat. I inspected my glass and was glad to see a healthy measure remained. We had left the bottle in a cooler bag back in the car, so a refill was out of reach. Fortunately, Matt had had the foresight to fill our glasses generously before we set off.

He took a sip and held his glass up to the sunlight. 'As a winemaker, the hallmarks of a great wine are balance and complexity. That's a massive part of what we aim for. I think we've achieved that with this wine. Perhaps this is bordering on being a great wine. Perhaps it *is* a great wine. I'll let others be the judge.'

I liked that my friend was proud. After all his hard work and endurance, I was glad to see him take pleasure in his creation. I thought of Van Gogh again. During his lifetime he received little recognition and was commonly written off as a crazy person. I doubted he could ever have anticipated the staggering influence his art would have upon the world. But I wondered if he enjoyed small moments of appreciation. On putting the finishing touches to such masterpieces as *The Starry Night* or *Café Terrace at Night*, did he take the time to marvel over his creations? Did he give himself permission to revel in the sunshine of his genius?

In the glow of the chardonnay, I found myself revelling on Van Gogh's behalf. I understood how great wine, like great art, could invoke a sensory experience. 'Learning to decode the different smells and tastes is much more fun than I imagined,' I said. 'I enjoy finding out about the different varieties and how they're made, but what I hadn't banked on was the way that wine opens things up.'

'How do you mean?'

'There's a pleasant place I arrive at when the alcohol's started to kick in, but I haven't drunk too much. It's a soft, worry-less feeling that comes when the low-grade anxiety of everyday life fades away. I find myself no longer dwelling on things like work or money or my waistline. My mind shifts into a more contemplative gear. I begin to consider life's bigger questions.'

Matt smiled approvingly. 'That's probably why there's such a strong connection between wine and philosophy. I bet many great philosophers spent their time talking and dreaming over bottles of wine.'

He was not wrong. In ancient Greece, thinkers would often share and discuss their ideas at ritual wine-drinking parties called 'symposia' (meaning, quite literally, 'drinking together'). Plato himself used one of these parties as the backdrop for his philosophical text *Symposium*. In *Symposium*, he portrays various notable figures of the time talking about the meaning and nature of love. Amid the conversation, the character of Pausanias complains of a hangover and warns fellow partygoers to take it easy. One of the revellers is Plato's own teacher, Socrates, the so-called 'father' of Western philosophy. As well as being celebrated for his wisdom, Socrates frequently attended symposia, and was famed for drinking heavily without ever appearing drunk. As far as Western philosophy is concerned, drinking and thinking went hand in hand from the very beginning. It was Plato who said: 'Nothing more excellent or valuable than wine was ever granted by the gods to man.'

More recently, the philosophers Simone de Beauvoir and Jean-Paul Sartre did their bit to keep the original spirit of the symposium alive. They were the original 'power couple' of 1950s French philosophy, and espoused the popular post-war theory of existentialism. They also knew how to party. They imbibed countless bottles of wine, whisky, vodka (the list goes on …) with the Parisian intellectual avant-garde. For them, intoxication was tied up with the existentialist approach of individuals defining their own sense of purpose in the face of life's apparent absurdity. Life might well be meaningless, but at least you could have a good time while living it! Granted, both Sartre and de Beauvoir developed cirrhosis of the liver later in life. They were not immune to alcohol's downsides.

I swirled my glass and considered the contradictions inherent in this seductive, golden liquid. 'There's so much to contemplate in wine,' I said. Matt raised an eyebrow, waiting for me to elaborate. 'There are all these colours, aromas and flavours that can transport you to other places and times. But that requires openness and imagination. Openness and imagination come more easily when you've had a glass or two. Wine softens your inhibitions and encourages your creative juices which, in turn, helps you better explore the qualities of the wine. It's almost as if wine *wants* you to appreciate it.'

There was a big smile on Matt's face. 'I love that idea! Many of the great things about wine are unlocked by the wine itself. It's like a Darwinian adaption.'

'If it is, it seems to be working well!' I raised my arms to indicate the abundance of evidence about us. While innumerable species of flora were being driven to extinction, the grapevine faced no such threat. We were standing in a landscape wholly designed and dedicated to the flourishing of *Vitis vinifera* (the common grapevine).

'To be fair, the grapevine probably would have survived without human help,' Matt pointed out. 'It's a remarkable weed insofar as it will just grow and grow and grow. But you're right that people have supported it along the way. I would say that humans and grapevines absolutely have a symbiotic relationship.'

My thoughts returned to Van Gogh's wheatfields, only this time from an anthropological angle. I had read about humanity's similarly strong links with wheat in the book *Sapiens: A Brief History of Humankind*, by the historian Yuval Noah Harari. 'He claims that one of the main reasons for the agricultural revolution was because wheat effectively manipulated human beings into growing and taking care of it.'

'What?!'

'I know it sounds a bit out there, but he makes a fairly interesting argument. For about two hundred thousand years, *Homo sapiens* were hunter-gatherers roaming the Earth and getting along quite well. Wheat, on the other hand, was just a specific variety of grass growing in a certain area of the Middle East. However, after wheat became domesticated ten thousand years ago, things started to change dramatically. Within a couple of thousand years, humans were largely settled down, and working harder than ever to look after their wheat plants. Wheat went global *because* it made human beings *dependent* on it. Arguably, humans didn't domesticate wheat – wheat domesticated humans.'

Matt's eyes grew wider as he considered the notion. I remembered having a similar reaction when I read *Sapiens*. The idea of a plant dominating humanity wasn't something I had ever entertained, outside of watching the musical comedy classic *Little Shop of Horrors*.

'Wow,' Matt said. 'Until this moment I'd only ever thought of humans cultivating grapevines, never the other way around. In fact, the wine grape made humans sit up and take notice of it. Therein lies the secret of its success. I would say over time we've become much more dependent on grapevines than they are on us.'

'Well, I suppose dependency is relative. Nobody really *needs* wine for their survival.'

'Speak for yourself!' Matt said with a chuckle. 'Although, in all seriousness, a lot of people do end up depending on it. That's a huge trap. There can be something truly wicked about alcohol in that respect.'

I nodded in agreement. I had witnessed first-hand the ravages of alcohol dependency. Alcoholism had the power to transform kindness into callousness, brilliance into derangement, love into loneliness. It could destroy families, squander talents and take lives. 'Wicked' was the right word.

But when I looked at the grapes hanging innocently on the vines, I couldn't see any wickedness. Each and every grape was entirely itself, pretending nothing and asking nothing. There were no malicious intentions or destructive impulses here.

There were just berries, simple and alive.

'Of course, alcohol is abused and that's obviously a horrible thing,' I replied. 'But the grapevine isn't complicit in that. It just wants to do what all plants do – survive and reproduce.'

'Very true.'

I took an easy mouthful of wine and let it sit on my palate for a few seconds. The flavours of peach and melon mingled with the faint taste of vanilla. With every sip I found something different. This chardonnay was kaleidoscopic. As with the grapes, it was difficult to find anything ill-intentioned in something so delightful.

'As far as I can tell, abuse of alcohol and appreciation of wine are entirely different things,' I said. 'When we overindulge it's usually about numbing or escaping or filling a void. If you are abusing alcohol, you're not trying to get the most out of it. You're trying to not be sober anymore. It has nothing to do with enjoyment or exploration.'

'But it's a fine line that can easily become blurred. How do you establish when you've stopped enjoying and started abusing?'

It was a good question. As someone who had never struggled with alcohol dependency, I felt unable to give a considered answer. I knew that for some it was best that they never drank a drop. For many others, their relationship with alcohol changed depending on their circumstances. The tendency towards overindulgence and reliance rose as the stressors of life increased. Then again, there were those fortunate individuals who possessed an entirely measured relationship with alcohol. They could enjoy their glass of wine without risk of virtue turning to vice. Humanity's relationship with alcohol was anything but clear-cut.

'To misquote Shakespeare,' I offered, 'wine isn't good or bad, but drinking makes it so. Or, to be more precise, your *reasons* for drinking play a major role in whether it's enhancing or destructive. What we've been talking about is how wine can help you think more deeply, relate more openly and consider things differently. To me, that has nothing to do with escaping life and everything to do with affirming life.'

'That's such an important point, because that's one of the things I most enjoy about sharing a bottle of wine. I love how it liberates conversation and gives you the ease to consider different points of view.'

Perhaps this was why Socrates was such a fan of conversing over wine. After all, he pioneered the 'Socratic method' – a style of debate founded in exploring ideas from multiple perspectives. He placed the emphasis on asking questions and investigating areas of ambiguity. He invited philosophers to challenge their own assumptions and explore alternative ways of seeing things. Maybe Socrates understood that the best way to achieve this was by being appropriately tipsy?

'Unfortunately,' I lamented, 'the ability to consider different points of view is in short supply these days. Most of us seem intent on aggressively defending our opinions and demonising people we disagree with.'

'I find strict adherence along ideological lines really lazy,' Matt said, with a look of frustration. 'All of us need to adapt our thinking as we encounter new information and circumstances. I love talking to people who have different ideas to me. Even if they don't change my mind, I almost always learn something.'

Matt was echoing the ideas of the philosopher Georg Hegel. The influential 19th-century German thinker described a process called 'dialectic', in which the encounter of opposing arguments led to the discovery of new concepts. 'Hegel was all about finding the sliver of truth in his opponent's position and adapting his thinking accordingly,' I told my friend.

'Great minds think alike!' said Matt. 'But where do you reckon this black-and-white thinking comes from? Why do we become so entrenched in our positions? Why are we so quick to attack ideas that challenge us?'

I looked out across the landscape, wondering. 'People's opinions can be unashamedly cruel or demeaning or bigoted. When that's the case, it's difficult *not* to get angry and defensive. Sometimes our ideas are wrapped up with our sense of identity, so when those ideas get challenged, we feel personally attacked. Egoism, social pressure, political tribalism, religious dogmatism – the list goes on. But regardless of the reason, more often than not I think the problem boils down to a lack of imagination.'

Matt gave me a curious look. 'Tell me more.'

'It's through imagination that we can put ourselves in another person's shoes. It's through imagination that we can escape the limitations of our own heads and experience empathy. Imagination is essential for not only understanding other people's views, but also understanding *why* they hold those views. If our first impulse is to shut down perspectives we can't relate to, we're likely not being very imaginative.'

The question of imagination was one I had given some thought. We live in an era of such easy amusement. Our phones and tablets and smart TVs serve a never-ending supply of content for consumption. With little need to rely on our own minds for entertainment, our creative faculties could well suffer from lack of exercise. If our imaginations are growing weak, what impact might this have on our capacity to connect with others? Do we run the risk of seeing the world in increasingly simple terms, without the colour and depth that imagination supplies?

'A curious, creative mind is just so important,' Matt said, taking the final sip from his glass. 'In fact, in winemaking, there's never been a more important time for imaginative problem-solving.'

'Why?'

'The changing climate. Wine growing and winemaking have always been unpredictable. The changing weather patterns are making things even harder to anticipate. You need to always be coming up with inventive solutions for whatever might come your way. But I don't mind having to find solutions on the fly. The creative aspect is one of the main reasons I love what I do.'

I finished my drink, holding the remaining chardonnay on my tongue for a moment to relish the flavour. Before I began this education, I wouldn't have thought of winemaking as a particularly creative pursuit. You grew the grapes, you crushed them, you put the juice in a barrel, and voila – wine! I had since learnt that imagination was at the heart of what Matt did. Winemaking was an art form. To be able to savour that art form, to taste it, now struck me as an incredibly evocative experience.

I quizzed Matt about the satisfaction to be found in knowing he had made a good wine. I imagined there must have been a catalogue of smells, flavours, feelings, thoughts and images that came to life, all of them reminiscent of the wine's creation, when he savoured his own success.

'Absolutely!' he said. 'I don't necessarily reflect on my own experiences in that way, but you're right on the money. I remember drinking one of my wines at a dinner party with friends. We had some major heat events the year of that vintage and I could detect the heat stress character in the wine. It stood out to me strongly. Even the distraction of everyone talking and eating didn't stop me from tasting the heat stress. It was all I could focus on.'

'What does heat stress taste like?'

'It's kind of bitter and harsh. It's like putting a collar on a dog's neck a little too tight. It constricts everything and dulls it down. It's like when a T-shirt has gone through the wash too many times and the colour has drained out.'

The entire time, I had been following Matt's lead as we made our way through corridors of leafy trellises. I was surprised to find we had returned to our starting place. As if shaken from a dream, I realised I had grown so absorbed in my thoughts that our surroundings had faded away into a hazy mirage. If someone had asked me to retrace our route, I would have been at a loss. I was a little sad that the spell had broken. There was something timeless, soft and safe about travelling in a daydream.

Matt pulled the cooler bag out of the car and replenished our glasses. We turned to look back over the vineyard as we began our second round.

'You've made me think about how much my memories are tied up with wine,' Matt said. 'When I taste or smell one of our wines, I can recall with an insane amount of detail the weather for that vintage. It's funny, because if you asked me to recall the details of some legal statute, I would have no hope.'

This didn't surprise me, given the neuroscience of memory. 'I'm no expert in this field, but a friend of mine who is told me that a direct connection had been found between the olfactory system and the parts of the brain responsible for forming memories and processing emotions. The olfactory system is responsible for smell and a lot of taste, which is why odours and flavours can easily bring up memories – particularly emotional ones.'

'Well, winemaking can be pretty emotional!' Matt let out a chortle. 'Here's another story for you. A few years back, a tap on one of our wine tanks failed to close fully, remaining slightly uncocked. This drained the tank overnight and we had to put in an insurance claim for the loss. When the insurance bloke came out to assess us, I could tell from his body language that he was sceptical. The thought bubble over his head could have read: "Yeah right, you guys are putting the wine down the drain and trying to pull off a fake claim." Well, I found myself launching into a twenty-minute-long monologue, detailing every vintage, showing him how important every wine was to us, telling him all about the rain and heat and grapevine diseases. He was blown away.'

'Which begs the question, what does an insurance claim taste like?' I asked, with a smirk.

'Delicious. We were paid out in full.'

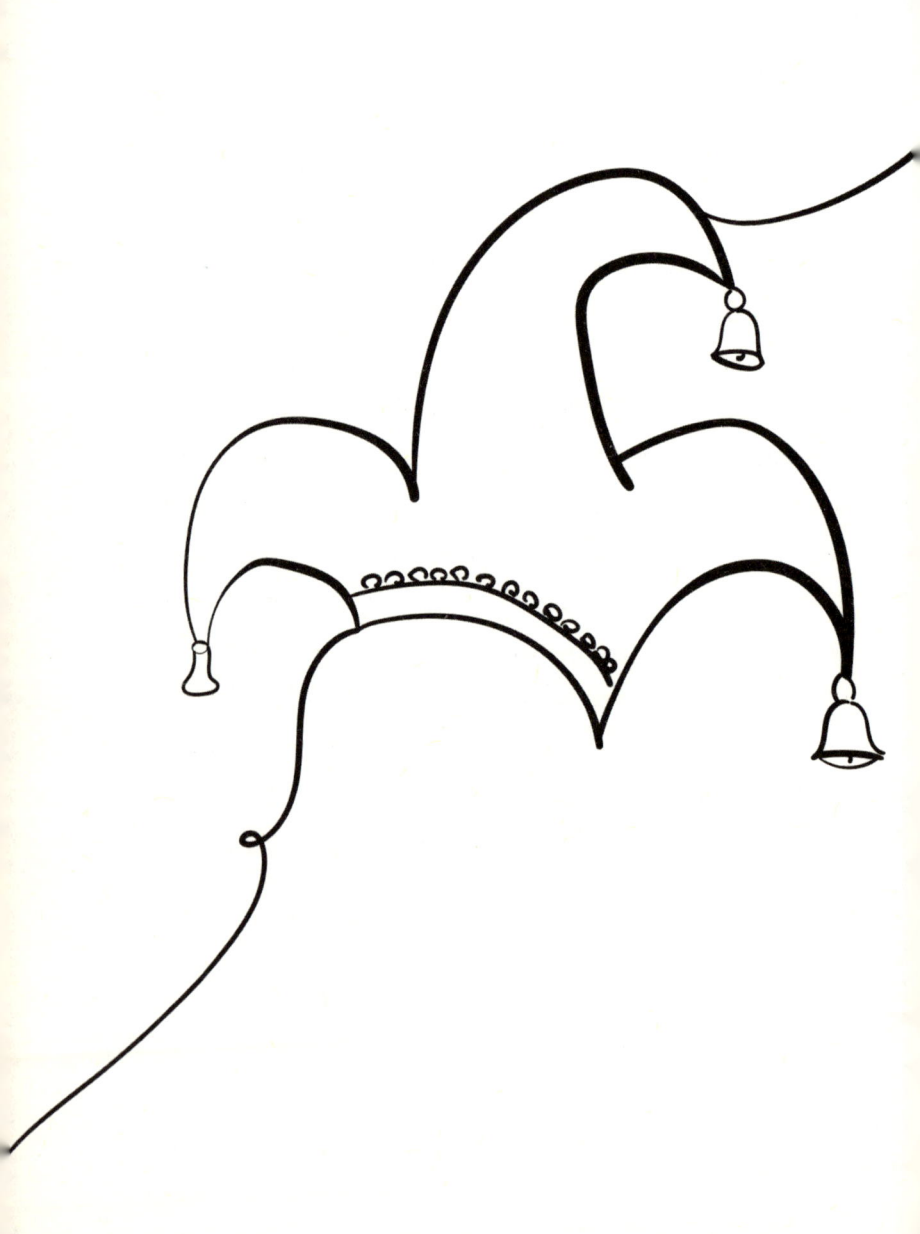

CHAPTER 5
Arneis

'What are your plans for the rest of the day?' Robert, my therapist, was looking at me with some concern. We had just finished a particularly fraught session, and I was a sodden mess.

'I'm tasting wine with a friend this afternoon,' I said.

'Sounds good.' Robert smiled reassuringly and reached out to shake my hand. I went to take his hand but realised I was holding a mess of crumpled, damp tissues. I stuffed the tissues in my pocket. We shook hands and I went to leave the office. As I walked out, I looked at one of the posters on the wall. It featured a boldly typed quote against the backdrop of a black-and-white landscape: 'Unexpressed emotions will never die. They are buried alive and will come forth later in uglier ways.'

Aristotle taught that the purpose of tragic theatre was to arouse feelings of 'pity and terror' in the audience, evoking catharsis – an ancient Greek medical term for 'cleansing' or 'purification'. Although exactly what Aristotle meant by this is up for debate, catharsis has come to describe the 'purifying' effect of experiencing raw and painful emotions. By becoming upset and feeling that upset fully, we 'cleanse' ourselves of emotional burdens. We come out the other side relieved and renewed.

I had experienced my fair share of catharsis on this day. It was true – I did feel better after an hour of crying. I also felt like sleeping for twelve hours. This was not unusual after my therapy with Robert. I was often surprised by how easily he cut to the quick. He was friendly, good-humoured, straight-talking and possessed a distinctly scientific world view. He was not someone I would have picked to bring grown men to tears on a regular basis. Nevertheless, he had a strange knack for pointing out those tender truths that broke my defences in a heartbeat.

Heading out into the cool autumn breeze, I boarded a tram and plonked myself heavily onto a seat. Tired. A week earlier, it had seemed like great time management to meet up with Matt directly after seeing Robert. Matt was staying in Melbourne for a couple of days and suggested that we go to one of his favourite wine bars in the city. The bar and Robert's clinic were in easy travelling distance. Nothing could be simpler. However, I had failed to factor in post-therapy exhaustion or post-crying eye puffiness. Did Matt really want to spend the afternoon with a wilted version of me; a drinking buddy who was neither lively nor glamorous?

I rallied. I had been looking forward to this catch-up all week. I was excited to see my friend and taste a wine variety I had never even *heard* of before, let alone tried. I would do my best to shift gears and try not to appear dishevelled. I was sure Matt wouldn't notice.

'Are you okay, mate?' Matt asked, after hugging me hello. 'You look a bit worse for wear.'

Evidently my acting skills needed work.

'I'm fine,' I replied. 'I just came from seeing my psychologist. It was quite the session.'

The wine bar had a decidedly European feel. The furniture and fittings were mostly made of dark and warmly lacquered wood. The chairs were bentwood, the type that cluttered Parisian cafes and cushioned the behinds of chain-smoking French intellectuals. There were several blackboards mounted on the walls, listing food specials and wine varieties carefully written in white chalk. A row of schoolhouse pendant lights hung from the ceiling above the bar, casting a golden, nostalgic glow.

'Let's get you a drink,' Matt said as we sat down. 'Sounds like you need one.'

He caught the eye of a waiter, who came quickly to our table. The waiter was tall, broadly built and had a finely manicured beard. He and Matt obviously knew one another. They shared friendly banter for a minute before Matt introduced me: 'Dale, this is my good friend Pete. I'm acting as his personal wine tutor. Today's lesson is arneis.'

Dale smiled, 'Ah, the little rascal!'

Matt ordered a bottle of white wine and a bowl of salted almonds. He asked if I'd like white anchovies to snack on as well. I declined. I didn't say so, but I found the idea of snacking on white anchovies horrifying.

'What did he mean when he said "the little rascal"?' I asked after Dale left.

'That's what they say the word arneis means – little rascal,' Matt said. 'I'm not sure whether it's true or not, but it certainly makes sense. Winemakers who grow arneis know what a rascal it can be. It's susceptible to disease and temperamental and messy. That's one of the reasons it's not grown widely in Australia. In fact, when we started growing it, I think it was the largest planting of arneis in Australia.'

'If it's so hard to deal with, why bother?'

Matt laughed. 'To be honest, I didn't really know what arneis was like when I planted it. I just knew I liked the wine. I had tried an excellent example in the King Valley that captured my imagination. I was in the mood to spread my winemaking wings. I think that's an integral part of the winemaking experience. You're never done. You have to keep trying new things.'

Dale returned with our wine and almonds. As the waiter poured, Matt explained that arneis was a northern Italian white wine variety from Piedmont. 'We're lucky to still have it because it nearly died out in the early 1970s. At the time, only two winemakers in the world were still making it. Nobody could be bothered, or so it seemed. Fortunately, it bounced back in the 1980s and, while it never became huge, it's now grown in vineyards in Italy, Australia and the US.'

Forgetting my wine-tasting etiquette, I dove straight into the aroma. Although not at once obvious, it had a nutty grittiness that immediately reminded me of almonds. It made sense that Matt had ordered a bowl of actual almonds to pair with the wine.

I tasted the wine and paused for a moment to consider. Matt awaited my assessment. I was stumped. It wasn't as if there was no flavour at all. Rather, it was a mix of hints and traces that I found difficult to pin down.

'I don't know what to say,' I confessed. 'This one's eluding me.'

Matt nodded. 'With "noble" wine varieties, like pinot noir or chardonnay, there are often more clearly pronounced aromas and flavours. It's easy to identify red plum or citrus or whatever it might be. I find Italian wine varieties aren't always like that – it can be harder to find overt characteristics.'

Matt explained that the 'noble' wines were traditionally considered the highest quality varieties. They were the 'classics'. Although consensus varied over which wines were noble, it was widely held that the top seven were cabernet sauvignon, merlot, pinot noir, riesling, sauvignon blanc, chardonnay and shiraz (or syrah, as the French call it).

'The noble varieties tend to be standalone. You can marvel at them in their own right, without needing to pair them with anything. I find Italian varieties are often more about texture, which means they can pair really well with food. I think that's interesting given how heavily food features in Italian culture.'

I took another sip, paying close attention to the mouthfeel. It felt warm. There was also a slight pull on the sides of my mouth, which Matt told me was 'grip'. Grip or 'structure' was generally considered a positive attribute in wine, Matt explained.

'The other thing that makes arneis hard to pin down is that there isn't a globally accepted style,' he said. 'Almost every arneis I've encountered tastes quite different.'

'It's a little rascal in more ways than one,' I remarked, finally taking time to consider the wine's colour. It was a light straw shade, not unlike the chardonnay we had shared. 'Not only is it hard to grow, but it defies categorisation. It's like one of those mythic trickster gods.'

The trickster was a common figure in mythologies the world over. Frequently portrayed as a male character and prone to taking the form of an animal, the trickster challenged authority and defied convention. Notable examples include the Norse god Loki, the Native American Coyote spirit and the African spider god Anansi. While the trickster might appear chaotic and destructive, its role was often to bring about new and better ways of being, through undermining the status quo.

'That's why I have a soft spot for arneis,' Matt said as he finished munching on a handful of almonds. 'Everyone in our winemaking team is always complaining about it, but to me it's a rough diamond. I think there's a lot more we could get out of it, but it has to be dealt with differently. Trying to control it doesn't work. It's a free spirit and you've got to respect that.'

I took an appreciative sip and offered up a term from the psychologist Carl Rogers: unconditional positive regard. 'He applied it to humans, but it seems to fit arneis well. The idea being that you show understanding and acceptance, regardless of what high jinks someone might get up to.'

'Exactly! You have to embrace the oddities, not resist them. It's like raising a kid. Trying to force them into a box doesn't work. You have to love them on their own terms.'

I winced. Our conversation was quickly veering into uncomfortable terrain; ground I'd covered in therapy only hours earlier.

Perhaps sensing my discomfort, Matt changed tack. 'An interesting fact about arneis is that it used to be planted as a "sacrificial grape". It was grown specifically to lure birds away from the more valuable nebbiolo grapes nearby. The arneis grapes ripened earlier and so birds would be drawn by their relative sweetness.'

As Matt described it, 'character' seemed the perfect word for arneis. It was 'quite the character', in the same way you might describe an aunt who collected cats, garden gnomes and turbans.

'Poor arneis,' I said. 'It's had quite a hard time.'

'That's true. But to be fair, it can be difficult to love. You can't really blame winemakers for not wanting to deal with it.'

I couldn't help but notice that the story of arneis flew in the face of our previous discussions, about grapevines and evolution. Wine flourished because humanity came to rely on it. Arneis seemed to do the opposite. It actively worked against humanity. There was something almost self-destructive about it.

Matt smiled knowingly. 'It certainly doesn't do itself any favours by making life so difficult for the humans trying to grow it!'

Dale returned to the table, asking if we needed anything else. As we declined, Dale pulled his right hand from behind his back to present a small chocolate torte with a single lit candle on top. Matt proceeded to sing 'Happy Birthday' to me.

'You shouldn't have!' I exclaimed. I blew out the candle. 'Thank you.'

'No worries, mate. Happy birthday.'

My birthday had been two weeks earlier. Mike and I had gone to our favourite lunch spot before catching up with some friends for dinner later that evening. It had been a lovely day. But the day after, I woke with a heavy feeling in my chest and difficult memories crowding my head. This was hardly surprising. I had come to expect a visit from the black dog of depression around this time of year. This had nothing to do with the season – I enjoyed the colder weather and auburn colours of autumn. Nor did it stem from a dislike of ageing or fears of mortality. Rather, it was the annual reminder that

I did not have parents who would light candles on a cake or sing Happy Birthday to me. The people who had given me my life did not care to celebrate it with me.

As the depression set in, my tendency was to turn against myself. *You're worthless – you do everything wrong – you always let down the ones you love.* In a more cheerful state, I could dismiss such distortions with ease. They simply weren't true. But when my mood darkened, I struggled. The thoughts were too constant and too loud, and I was too tired to fight them. After a week of feeling chest-deep in crude oil, I had given Robert a call.

Now, as Matt and I sampled this strange, new wine, I was eager to evade the spotlight. I asked how Matt was faring, embarrassed that I hadn't asked sooner.

'I'm well thanks, mate. Busy – really, really busy.'

Negotiating three young daughters, a vineyard and a cellar door construction job was proving more than a little time-consuming.

'Thank goodness for Lu,' he said. 'She's the most amazing mum to the kids – patient, kind and always makes time. Poor thing is so tired and constantly in demand. As far as I'm concerned, the medals and trophies shouldn't go to the wines we make. They should go to Lu.'

The building work was progressing nicely. 'It's good fun. I like dealing with the daily challenges and we're working with a fantastic team. It's just hard to manage priorities.'

'Aren't you also in the middle of harvest?' I remembered him telling me that the grapes were harvested in March and April.

'That's right. Hopefully I will only say this once in my life, but harvest is a lower priority for me at the moment. I've had to be less involved this year. There's only one Matt!'

There was indeed only one Matt, and I was relieved that role was his and not mine. As much as Matt found a life of plate-spinning and problem-solving invigorating, his to-do list made me want to hyperventilate into a paper bag.

'But I want to hear about you,' he said. 'Is everything okay?'

I briefly detailed my post-birthday blues and the unfriendly workings of my mind. 'Talking of arneis being self-destructive, I can definitely relate. When I feel bad, I tend to pick on myself relentlessly. It's like having an abusive prison guard patrolling my brain.'

'I'm sorry to hear you've been feeling that way.'

I waved a hand in the air dismissively.

'You know, I feel for arneis,' I said. 'It's been hung out to dry as a sacrificial grape and it's almost as if it deliberately misbehaves in response. Of course, I know that's not how plants work, but it reminds me of a delinquent kid who acts out because they feel unloved.'

Matt nodded. 'It's a good analogy.'

'There's a saying: "Hurt people hurt people." Often when we feel rejected, our impulse is to reject back. It's defensive. I've been guilty of that myself. There was a time when I even pushed friends away – not because of anything they did, but because I was afraid that they would want to push me away. I acted pre-emptively. I rejected them before they had a chance to reject me.'

'Why would you assume people would want to reject you?'

I shrugged. 'I suppose when your own parents don't accept you, a belief is planted that everyone else will do the same. I know it's not rational, but shame can be very persuasive.'

After Dale had topped up our glasses once more, I changed the subject with a little nod to the cheeky spirit of arneis. 'Have you ever noticed that Dale is really handsome?' I asked with a smile.

Matt laughed. 'You just like him because he gives you cake! Yeah, he's a good-looking man and a top bloke too. They're great supporters of our wines here.'

I turned to the expansive collection of wine bottles populating one wall of the bar. A thick oak ladder leant against the shelves, reminding me of the rail ladders used in stately libraries. I wondered aloud if the wines on the top-shelf were indeed 'top-shelf'.

'I think so,' Matt said, squinting to make out the uppermost labels. 'Of course, you have to be careful about assuming that the more expensive wines are also the best. There are some fantastic wines that are very affordable, and some high-priced wines that are fairly disappointing. While price can be a decent indicator of quality, it isn't always.'

'Good to know.'

Matt took a healthy mouthful of arneis. 'You've got me thinking about the kind of self-destructive behaviour I engage in. For me, it's more about getting into unhealthy habits, like overindulging when I'm under stress, and not exercising. Eating badly and, so, weight gain, becomes a big one for me. I've always struggled with my weight, and I hate it.'

I remembered Matt telling me about his weight problems when we met in Florence. At the time I had difficulty reconciling the athletically built young man in front of me with the overweight schoolboy he described. I was incredulous when he told me that he had been bullied mercilessly for being fat. It was only when he showed me photos of his adolescent self that I understood. Before he had grown into a lean high-school rowing champion, he was a pudgy-faced and self-conscious kid. Matt hadn't always lived the life of success and social acceptance I had imagined.

'Speaking of weight gain,' Matt said, picking up one of the two cake forks that Dale had left for us, 'let's try this torte.'

In no time, we had demolished the small, neatly round cake. Rich and velvety, the bittersweet chocolate filling was delicious. I closed my eyes, focusing solely on the flavour. All my troubles seemed to melt away.

'Good, isn't it?' Matt grinned as I opened my eyes.

'Fabulous! A much better option than white anchovies.'

'Hey, there's nothing wrong with an anchovy!' He wiped

his lips with a napkin and looked away thoughtfully. 'I once discussed the topic of self-destructiveness with a doctor friend. He said that people are more likely to engage in self-destructive behaviour when major life events occur, even positive ones. They leave home, get married, get a promotion or whatever else it might be, and they experience a certain emptiness. Their achievements don't bring the satisfaction they're after and they can respond in harmful ways.'

I knew it well. More than once in my life I had worked tirelessly towards a particular end, hoping that it might finally fill that hollowness inside. But no matter how many titles and accomplishments I accrued, the outer trappings of 'success' had never brought peace of mind. It had taken me a long time to realise that fulfilment required a different approach.

'It comes back to self-worth,' I said. 'Looking back, I realise that I often pursued goals not because of what I wanted, but to prove my worth. I was trying to build an identity rather than live an authentic life. When the goals didn't bring me what I was after, or I experienced failure, the underlying sense of unworthiness would bubble to the surface. That's when the self-destructiveness really kicked in.'

'I've one hundred per cent seen that with mates of mine. Something big happens, good or bad, and they start to unravel. They drink heavily or do drugs or break up with their girlfriend for no apparent reason. Wouldn't it be better to deal with the actual problem and work on their self-esteem?'

'Of course,' I replied. 'But oftentimes people aren't aware of what the actual problem *is*. They have no real understanding of the motives that drive them. I think this is particularly true for men because they are taught from a young age to cut themselves off from their feelings. They often have no idea how to respond to emotional turmoil, so they react impulsively. As you say, they break up with their girlfriend even though their problem has nothing to do with the girlfriend – they just feel strange and don't know what to do about it.'

In the late 19th century, the famed Austrian neurologist Sigmund Freud popularised the concept of the 'unconscious mind'. According to Freud, many of our problems are rooted in feelings, perceptions, phobias and desires, of which we are not consciously aware. While much of what Freud taught has since been discredited, the idea of the 'unconscious' has evolved over time and remains widely accepted. As it turns out, it is not only difficult to grasp another person's thoughts or intentions – it is hard to comprehend our own.

I recalled a book I had read at university, *Strangers to Ourselves,* by the philosopher Julia Kristeva. 'It talks about the idea of the foreigner, and how it isn't just someone from another country or whose lifestyle we don't understand. We are also foreigners to ourselves. There are always parts of who we are that we aren't comfortable with or can't entirely fathom. I don't believe that's a problem in and of itself. I think problems arise depending on how we *treat* the difficult or unacknowledged aspects of ourselves. Do we treat them like a welcomed guest or a hostile invader? We can always try to be hospitable to strangers, even if we don't understand them. The same is true for ourselves. But if we go to war with the parts of ourselves that we find strange or unacceptable, that's when we get into trouble. That is, by definition, self-destructive.'

Matt had been listening patiently, consistently emptying his glass in the process. I had delivered this monologue more for my own benefit than for his. I had not been treating myself like a welcomed guest of late. Quite the opposite. It was time to declare a ceasefire and invite myself in for a cup of tea. I was sure Robert would approve.

'I really like that idea of welcoming yourself,' Matt said. 'That was basically how I managed to control my weight over the past year. Rather than being hard on myself and getting super restrictive with my diet, I focused on my mental and physical health day by day. If one evening I ate or drank too much, I didn't make a big deal out of it. I just moved on and did my best to keep taking care of myself.'

I had noticed Matt's weight loss, but it was a rule of mine to never comment on such things. For me, complimenting someone on their weight loss logically implied that they had looked bad *before* they lost the weight.

Matt continued: 'I also notice that when I'm kinder to myself, I'm kinder to others. When I'm burnt out, I don't like the way I am with my family or the guys at work. When I look after myself, I'm a much better husband, dad and boss.'

'I know exactly what you mean,' I said. 'I cringe when I think about the times I've been really stressed out and people around me got caught in the crossfire. If we're not treating other people with care and consideration, it's an important prompt to look at how we're treating ourselves.'

Matt gestured to the empty wine bottle on the table. 'So, what does this all say about our friend arneis?'

'What it says to me is that you have just the right attitude towards arneis. You accept and appreciate it for what it is. You welcome it.'

'Well, I try,' Matt said. 'It's not always easy. But I suppose if it was easy, everyone would do it.'

'Exactly.' I finished my glass. 'In a way, we're all like arneis. No matter how hard we work on ourselves, we can all be temperamental and messy and difficult to handle. The same is true for other people and for life in general. Things don't go the way we want them to, and we can never tie up all the loose ends. But that's the challenge, isn't it? Continually greeting everything and everyone on their own terms – including ourselves. We don't have to always like it, but we can learn to work with what we've got.'

Dale walked over to clear the table. Matt gave me a wink and I rolled my eyes in return. No doubt my comment about Dale's handsomeness would come back to haunt me.

Turning to me, Dale asked, 'How did the lesson go? What did you learn?'

'Lots of things. I learnt what a noble variety is, that arneis nearly died out in the 1970s and that "grip" is good. But the main lesson was that even though arneis is difficult to grow, it is worth the effort.'

'I'd agree with that,' Dale replied. 'It's great that we've got winemakers who are prepared to put in the hard yards.'

I smiled. The dense, foggy feeling of the past weeks had evaporated. I was sitting in an unfamiliar wine bar, filled with people I had never met, and yet I couldn't have felt more at home.

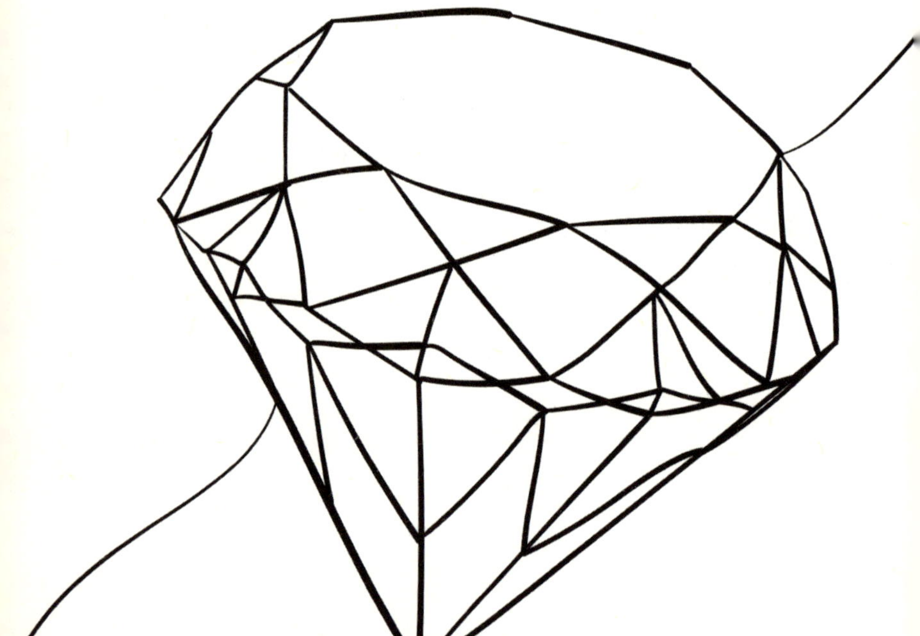

CHAPTER 6
Sangiovese

As we got up to leave the wine bar, Matt's phone rang: 'Sorry mate, I've got to take this.'

Left to chat to Dale the waiter, I learnt he was studying for the Advanced Sommelier exam, one rank below 'Master'. He explained that for this exam a lot of emphasis was placed on 'service' – presenting impeccable wine lists, effortlessly uncorking bottles, correctly positioning glasses and generally being a delight. Before I could embarrass myself by telling Dale that his service was *amazing* and I was sure he would pass with flying colours, Matt tapped me on the shoulder. It was time to go.

'That was my appointment for this evening getting cancelled,' Matt explained as we passed the stately theatre next door to the bar. 'It's a shame because we were booked for dinner at one of my favourite spots in the city. I'll have to cancel the booking. Unless you're free?'

With Mike out that evening, my plan had been to have beans on toast.

'I can probably free up my schedule,' I said.

'Fantastic!' he replied. 'Actually, that gives me an idea. Wait here.'

Matt dashed back inside the wine bar. I passed the time gazing at the London plane trees lining the street. I saw that their leaves were starting to turn yellow. I looked forward to seeing them darken and fall from their branches, dancing along the path in gusts of icy air as darkly dressed pedestrians hurried by. There was something so beautifully melancholic about Melbourne in autumn, like a poem by Robert Frost or a song by Billie Holiday.

Matt returned holding a bottle wrapped in a brown paper bag.

'I grabbed a bottle of our sangiovese,' he announced. 'We're going to have two lessons in one day!'

Matt's favoured dining spot was a well-regarded Italian restaurant, specialising in regional cuisine and seasonal produce. Decorated with white-washed brick walls and rustic furniture, it was located in a former warehouse basement. As was so often the case in Melbourne, it was a tucked-away gem that I had walked past many times without ever knowing it was there.

'Do you remember drinking sangiovese in Florence?' Matt asked after the waitress had finished pouring our glasses.

Before heading to Italy, I had read up on a rare psychosomatic condition called 'Stendhal syndrome'. Named after the 19th-century author Marie-Henri Beyle (better known by the nom de plume 'Stendhal'), the syndrome is induced by exposure to great art. In a record of his travels to Florence, Stendhal had recounted a visit to the Basilica of Santa Croce. There, he was overcome by the splendour of Giotto's frescoes, and almost passed out. Like Stendhal, hundreds of visitors to Florence were recorded as having art-induced breakdowns.

Although I never suffered from a bout of Stendhal syndrome, Florence's magnificent art and architecture left a lasting impression. Mostly my recollections of the city were of grand facades, timeless artworks and painterly streetscapes. I also vividly recalled many wonderful meals, but as for wine – not so much.

'I remember wine being served with pretty much every meal,' I replied. 'But I'd be lying if I said I was paying attention.'

'Let's see if we can jog your memory,' Matt said.

Sangiovese was named for the Latin 'sanguis Jovis' – the blood of Jupiter. Just as Jupiter was king of the ancient Roman gods, sangiovese had ruled the vineyards of Tuscany for hundreds of years.

'They can date back sangiovese to the sixteenth century, although it's probably much older,' Matt said. 'Some even think it was grown by the Etruscans, more than two thousand years ago. Either way, it's been the top Italian wine variety for a long time.'

The wine was richly red in colour. It smelt of roses and old leather.

'Like arneis, I think of sangiovese more in terms of texture than aroma or flavour,' Matt explained. 'Our region makes wines that are quite aromatic, so this one has a stronger aroma than you might find in Tuscan examples.'

The moment I tasted it, I realised I was a liar. I could absolutely remember drinking sangiovese in Florence. Suddenly I was sitting in a bustling restaurant not far from the Duomo, drinking wine as I laughed with friends. It was the flavour of red-and-white checked tablecloths, crusty bread drizzled with olive oil, and wanderlust.

Matt laughed at this revelation. 'I was hoping that would happen,' he said.

I told him I remembered finding it easy to drink the wine in Italy because it was quite light. 'I would almost describe it as watered down, although that sounds bad.'

Matt nodded reassuringly. 'I know exactly what you mean. Sangiovese is typically medium-bodied and naturally high in acid. That combination gives it a lighter, fresher feel. In new-world winemaking, we typically make sangiovese in a richer and denser style. However, I personally prefer the lighter style of the old world. I feel it's truer to character.'

Having heard Matt use the terms 'new world' and 'old world' before, I had done a little homework on what they meant. I learnt that the old world was synonymous with the long-standing wine traditions of Europe. It was here that the rules of modern winemaking were established. Old-world countries included France, Italy, Spain and Germany. The new world referred to those countries that inherited their winemaking traditions from the old world through colonisation. New-world wine regions included South America, North America, South Africa, New Zealand and Australia. Where the old world made the rules, the new world bent, broke and changed them. Naturally, these different approaches to winemaking, combined with the variation in climates and landscapes, resulted in characteristically distinct wines. Many of the old-world wines were lower in alcohol, higher in acid, lighter-bodied and subtle. New-world wines were often higher in alcohol, lower in acid, fuller-bodied and bold. 'Old' and 'new' was a neat tool for classifying the geography of wine.

However, the deeper I dug the more I realised that things weren't so clear-cut. While some classed countries such as Armenia, Turkey, Georgia, Israel, Iran and Lebanon as 'old world', others categorised them as 'ancient world'. Then there were places like Greece, Slovenia and China, which were variously categorised as 'ancient world', 'new old world' and 'new world' depending on who you listened to. Wine had been produced in numerous places across the globe for approximately eight thousand years, flourishing and diminishing in various regions with the ebb and flow of history. Differentiating the 'old' from the 'new' could be like deciding which way was up in an Escher drawing. When it came to wine, there were worlds within worlds.

With the sangiovese on my tongue, and the many worlds of wine spinning before me, I had another revelation.

'When we started out, the idea of travelling *through* wine was such an abstract concept,' I said. 'This is the first time it's felt real for me.'

'The French use the term "terroir",' Matt said. 'There isn't an exact English translation, but it broadly means the sense of place. Terroir encompasses everything from the soil to the type of vine to the climate to the winemaking culture. The better you come to know wine, the more that sense of place will shine through.'

The waitress arrived with our primi dishes. She presented plates of fried zucchini flowers stuffed with ricotta, and heirloom tomatoes with buffalo mozzarella and basil. When she wished us 'buon appetito', I looked up to thank her and noticed the tiredness in her eyes.

'Busy week?' I asked.

'You could say that,' she replied warmly. 'My boyfriend and I got engaged yesterday, so there was lots of celebrating.'

'Congratulations!' Matt and I said in unison. We asked a cavalcade of questions. Our waitress, whose name was Julia, had gone with her boyfriend James on a hot-air-balloon ride over the Yarra Valley. He had proposed to her two thousand feet in the air, with the same engagement ring that his great-great-grandfather had given to his great-great-grandmother. It was a filigree silver ring centred with a large emerald surrounded by rose cut diamonds.

'It's a good thing that James's great-great-grandfather had such excellent taste,' I said.

She laughed, looking lovingly at the ring. 'You're not wrong. I dread to think what James would have chosen if left to his own devices. I better get going, guys. Wave if you need anything.' Julia hurried away.

'Isn't that cool?' said Matt. 'An heirloom passed down through the generations like that.'

As Matt tucked into the fried zucchini flowers, I contemplated the glass of wine in front of me.

'There's a Buddhist scripture called the *Avatamsaka Sutra*,' I said, thinking carefully as I spoke. 'It describes an infinitely large net belonging to the Hindu god Indra. Each crossing point in the net is set with an exquisite, multifaceted jewel. Each jewel in the net reflects every other jewel in the net, so that all the jewels reflect all the other jewels ad infinitum. It's a metaphor for the Buddhist concept of "pratityasamutpada", which translates as "dependent arising".'

Matt chuckled. 'I love that this is our dinner conversation. Please go on.'

'Well, the idea is that everything comes into being dependent on other causes. Nothing exists on its own – it coexists with everything else. The wine we're drinking is a perfect example. For hundreds of years, people have been growing and making this wine. Think of all the lives and labour that have gone into keeping this tradition alive, not to mention the natural elements like the seasons and soil. Then think about those people who travelled across the oceans to Australia, bringing the sangiovese grape with them. Then there's you, who chose to grow and make sangiovese. That was only possible because of the land and the support of the people you work with. I could go on and on, but you get the drift.'

He did. 'Then there's you and me meeting in Florence all those years ago,' Matt said, 'which led to us sharing this bottle of wine tonight.'

'Exactly so. This wine and our friendship, which originated on the other side of the world, is the outcome of innumerable causes coming together in just the right way. When you think about it, it's breathtaking. No wonder the Buddhists described interdependence as a web of reflecting jewels. The value of enjoying this glass of wine with a good friend is a reflection of so much more than you and me and seven hundred and fifty millilitres of red grape juice.'

I spooned some slices of tomato and cheese onto my plate.

'I love that idea of a thing's value being tied up with its history and connection with other causes,' Matt said, his face lighting up. 'It's something I think really distinguishes wine as a beverage. Wine takes an extraordinary amount of time to make, and so much has to go right along the way. There're also so many people involved in its creation, from the cooper making the barrel to the viticulturist tending the vines to the winemaker overseeing the pressing, fermentation, maturation and bottling. Then, of course, there's Mother Nature, who can make or break a vintage depending on her mood.'

Since beginning our wine lessons, I had grown accustomed to how Matt spoke about Mother Nature. He described her in religious terms – as a goddess who was at once kind and cruel, whose favour or fury was his constant concern. But Mother Nature wasn't an abstract object of faith for him. She was a living presence who demanded reverence and regard.

I said as much to him. I remarked that the way he talked about Mother Nature made me think of a Celtic druid. He laughed.

'She's my boss!' he said. 'I have to treat her with respect. If she cracks the shits, I know about it.'

He was proving my point perfectly. The ancient pagan gods and goddesses were often depicted as complex characters. They had changing moods, flights of fancy, conflicts and dramas. Perhaps that was because ancient people had a closer awareness of the changeable nature of things. They were much more exposed to the caprice of the elements than we are today. And yet, external forces still play an enormous part in our lives. I told Matt about how, over the years, I had given considerable thought to how significantly our lives are shaped by elements – be they weather, or otherwise – beyond our control. I had often wondered how I might have coped if I had lived in, say, Nigeria or Saudi Arabia as a gay man. The Fates apportioned their gifts and penalties according to a logic I could not understand.

'Not to take away from our own efforts,' I said, 'but both of us have been amazingly blessed by circumstances we had no hand in creating.' I gestured to indicate our surroundings. 'Look at where we are – enjoying beautiful food and wine in a lovely restaurant. This is a luxury so many people could only ever dream of. The fact that we met in *Florence* while furthering our university education is all the evidence we should ever need that we are very lucky men.'

Working in the charity sector, it was difficult to forget my privilege. What many of us take for granted – proper sanitation, health care, education, an abundance of food – is unavailable to *millions* of human beings. I had realised long ago that having a stocked pantry, a flushing toilet or access to a hospital were reasons enough to be thankful.

'Absolutely,' Matt confirmed. 'I've had so many advantages in life, and I try to make the most of them. I'm particularly grateful to my family for all the support and opportunities they've given me.'

I noted that one of the oldest forms of religious devotion is ancestor worship. You see it in cultures all over the world. For example, it's not uncommon in modern-day Chinese households for there to be an altar dedicated to relatives who have passed away. The spirits of the ancestors are venerated for all the blessings they handed down to the living. There's such a wonderful sense of continuity there. It's an acknowledgement and celebration of the legacy every individual owes to their forebears. In my travels I had seen such altars first-hand, adorned with fruits, flowers, and photographs. It was touching to witness the care with which descendants gave offerings and made prayers. I remembered being taught about 'ghost money' – brightly coloured pieces of paper burnt for the benefit of the ancestors, ensuring they had plenty of currency to enjoy in the afterlife. I found this blurring of the line between the living and the dead strangely comforting, a reminder that love could continue.

I was reminded too of the debt I owed to my own forebears. Although our relationship had fallen apart, I couldn't help recognising all that my parents had done for me. They had worked hard to give me a good education and quality of life. In so many ways, they had forsaken their own needs in deference to mine. As much as there had been hurt and rejection, I didn't want to forget the care with which I was raised. Over time, I had learnt that I could be grateful to my parents without their cooperation.

Matt chewed pensively. Clearly my mention of ancestor worship had hit home.

'I think a lot about my own legacy,' he said gently. 'I know it sounds clichéd, but I see myself as a custodian of the land. That's one of the reasons I like to work with nature rather than pump it with fertilisers or manage it with sprays. I want the land I care for to be in the best possible condition for whoever inherits it, regardless of whether my kids choose to take it over or not.'

I was struck by this remark. Matt saw himself as an ancestor-in-the-making. He understood that his actions would echo into the future, shaping the fortunes of his successors.

'There's something quite profound in that idea of legacy,' I said. 'Nowadays we're preoccupied by the archetype of the self-made person concerned with their own wealth, career and success. The focus is very much on what we as individuals can accomplish in the here and now. We're not really taught to consider those who came before us *or* those who will come after us. As a result, I don't think we pay nearly enough attention to the long-term consequences of what we do for short-term gain.'

Julia arrived and went about picking up the empty plates. I was surprised to realise that Matt and I had demolished both servings of appetisers. Evidently, my attention had been on the conversation and not on the food. I was determined to give more awareness to the second course.

'You gentleman enjoying yourselves?' Julia asked.

We nodded enthusiastically. I asked whether she and James had discussed when they might get married.

'Pretty soon,' she said. 'One of things that gave James the courage to pop the question was the fact that his mum is unwell. We obviously want her to attend the wedding, so the sooner the better.'

'I'm sorry to hear that,' I replied.

Julia gave a small shrug. 'Nothing much to be done, unfortunately. We just want to show her the best time possible. She's an amazing lady.' She smiled. 'I'll get your main course sorted.'

Julia left and I turned to Matt. 'That's a sad reason to plan a wedding.'

Matt took a sip of wine. 'It is. As we've been saying, there's so much in life that's outside our control. I guess Julia and James are making the best of the cards they've been dealt.'

I told Matt that the ancient Stoic philosophers would have approved. 'They said that true contentment is found in focusing exclusively on what is within our control. Most of us like to think that we can control so much more than we can. According to the Stoics, the only things we can genuinely control are our own actions, perceptions and reactions. The rest is not our business, and we shouldn't worry about it.'

'It's like a winemaker complaining about the weather,' Matt said. 'There's literally *nothing* you can do to change the weather. Worrying about it is just stressful and pointless. In fact, I think it diminishes your ability to make good decisions when Mother Nature throws things upside down.'

There she was again. Mother Nature, Matt's goddess.

'That's the interesting thing about the control freaks I've known,' I said. 'As I've gotten to know them, I've always realised how out of control they are within themselves.

Although they might project a veneer of dominance, they feel powerless and afraid – which is why they try to control all the people and events around them. In my experience, the most powerful people don't try to dominate others – they focus on what's within their control, and lead through example.'

'That's something I really focus on as a parent,' Matt replied. 'Showing my kids the best example I have to offer.'

I had noticed a slight shift in my friend's demeanour when he mentioned his children. His features softened, and his eyes became gentle. Now he had me wondering – what had winemaking taught him about being a parent?

'Winemaking has taught me a lot about being a nurturer,' he said. 'The way to get the best out of a vine is to be sensitive to its needs and nurture its best qualities. The same is true with kids. You have to nurture and guide them according to *their* nature, not yours.'

I wanted to give him a hug, but I just smiled instead. 'So, in a sense, control is the opposite of connection. In my experience, true connection comes when I drop my expectations for the other person. It's only then that I can relate to them in a genuine way. If I'm trying to control or change someone, I'm not really connecting with them. I'm connecting with my idea of how they *should* be.'

Matt had a distant look in his eye as he responded. 'Control is the opposite of connection. I really think there's something in that. I feel so much more connected to my

Sangiovese

kids when I embrace who they are. For me, parenting, like winemaking, is about surrendering to the process of life. My kids are these beautiful beings who are travelling with me through life. I help them out when I can, and they help me more than I can say.'

My dear friend was starting to tear up. I began to do the same. I handed him a napkin. We looked at each other and laughed. Two big men crying in an Italian restaurant. The sangiovese was obviously taking effect.

'Here we go, gentlemen,' Julia announced, as two plates of steaming pasta arrived. 'Can I get you some cracked pepper?'

We turned to her.

'Am I interrupting something?' she asked, taken aback by our dewy eyes.

I laughed. 'No, your timing is perfect. Cracked pepper would be lovely. Thank you.'

Matt explained to Julia that he had been talking with me about how amazing his kids are – hence the feelings.

'Kids are the best,' she said, grinding the top of the oversized wooden pepper mill. 'I've got a little boy of my own. He's such a champion.'

'What's his name?' I asked.

'Jackson,' she replied. 'We're a family of J's.'

She told us that Jackson had been so excited by the engagement that he couldn't stop hugging James. James had asked Jackson for his blessing beforehand, so Jackson knew what was coming. The boy had been brimming with anticipation for James to finally pop the question.

'James isn't Jackson's biological dad, but the two get along famously,' Julia said. 'It was actually seeing how good James was with Jackson that made me decide he was the one.'

Attempting to make a poetic observation about continuity, I remarked that maybe one day Jackson might use Julia's ring to propose to his own fiancée.

'Maybe,' she responded. 'Provided that he falls in love with a woman. He might be gay, in which case I don't think this ring would work. He's obsessed with *Hairspray* and *Frozen,* so I've started to wonder.'

I chortled. My endeavour to make a grand narrative of the situation had fallen flat. Julia had caught me out in my own assumptions. It never failed to amaze me the way younger parents were so carefree when it came to the question of their children's sexual orientation. What had once been so taboo was now so normal as to be hardly worth mentioning. If only my parents had shared this sentiment.

Julia again wished us 'buon appetito', before departing.

Matt had ordered potato gnocchi with beef ragout, and I had ordered spinach and ricotta ravioli. As I took my first bite, I was surprised by the flavour. I cut open a pasta envelope to see that the ravioli was in fact stuffed with *bacon* and ricotta.

'We'll send it back,' Matt said, immediately turning to hail Julia back to the table.

'No, no,' I replied. 'Leave it. I'll enjoy the meal I have. Tonight's all about trusting in fate.'

He raised his glass. 'I'll drink to that. Here's to surrendering control!'

'Here's to letting go!'

CHAPTER 7
Pinot Grigio

When I first met Matt on our Italian study tour, I had assumed he was a man untroubled by life's difficulties. He seemed implacably confident and well placed, at ease with everyone and always up for an adventure. I compared his apparent blessings with my own shortcomings. Where he was the epitome of cheerful self-assurance, I was a mess of anxieties. Where he had comfortably enjoyed a relationship with the same girlfriend for years, I was struggling with my sexuality and had never been kissed. Where he had been a championship-winning member of his school's rowing team, I was woefully uncoordinated and had always been chosen last for any school sports. He was the textbook example of everything that would make a parent proud. Why couldn't I be more like Matt? Why couldn't I stroll through life in the sunshine of the world's approval?

It did not take long for me to realise that my story of Matt was missing some important plot points. We were seated next to each other on a bus ride back to Florence following a day trip. As the sky darkened over the countryside, we discussed our charming afternoon wandering Siena's circling medieval cityscape. After exchanging anecdotes of magical alleyways, grand piazzas and delicious biscotti, the conversation turned to the topic of Matt's family. I learnt that his father was the founder of a major auction house. It was clear that he held his parents in high regard.

'Mum and Dad are both incredibly hard-working,' he said. 'I have a huge amount of respect for what they've achieved. It sets an important standard for me and my brothers to live up to. I often think about that. I don't want to be a disappointment.'

I couldn't imagine anybody calling this charismatic young law student a disappointment, and I told him so.

'Well, certainly Mum and Dad have never said that,' he replied. 'It's more something I say to myself.'

'Do *you* think you're a disappointment?' I asked, taken aback.

He glanced out the bus window. 'I sometimes feel guilty about not working as hard as I could at uni. I've been extremely fortunate in life, and I want to be worthy of the opportunities I've been afforded. I worry I'm not achieving enough, which makes me worry I'm letting my folks down.'

On reflection, it was only natural that someone with successful parents might feel obligated to live up to their example. It was also understandable that Matt was eager to earn his own place in the world. What took me by surprise was the realisation that *nobody*, not even my friend Matt, was free from anxieties and self-doubt. It was something I would be reminded of time and again as I travelled through life – no matter how blessed or socially acceptable or well adjusted a person might seem, they are not immune to the quirks of the human soul. This was perhaps the first lesson that Matt ever taught me.

Little could I have imagined on that meandering bus drive through Tuscany that almost two decades later, Matt would be giving me a lesson of an entirely different variety in his newly renovated cellar door. There was no guessing at the time that Matt would ever own a cellar door to renovate in the first place.

'Okay,' Matt was saying as he poured from a bottle of white wine. It was late autumn, and his cellar door renovation project was finally finished. 'This is a confusing wine. The grape is called pinot gris, and it's one of only a few varieties that presents as a different colour on the vine to how it presents in the glass.'

'What do you mean?'

'It's a white wine but it can have quite a dark pink skin as a grape. This is a sweeping generalisation, but the French do a style of pinot *gris* that is luscious, round and soft. The Italians use the same grape but make it in the pinot *grigio* style, which is fresh and racy.'

'So, you make it in the Italian style,' I said, gesturing to the bottle on the table marked 'Pinot Grigio' in a bold art deco font.

'Not quite. We call this pinot grigio, but if we were to place it on a spectrum between the French style and the

Italian style, this would be somewhere in the middle. Ours has some roundness and softness of pinot gris, but also has the underlying fresh acid drive of the pinot grigio.'

'The best of both worlds.'

'I think so,' he said, with a cheeky grin.

We were seated in the tasting room, which had as its centrepiece a sizeable bar with a butcher's rail above it. Warmly glowing vintage light bulbs hung from twined green chords along the rail. The perimeter of the room was lined with large windows, affording an effortless view of the garden and surrounding sky. The view was complemented by the high, white-washed ceiling which provided a generous sense of space. The airy, open atmosphere made this somewhere to easily while away the hours in lubricated conversation.

Matt had already given me a guided tour of the garden, describing the plant varieties with the pride of a loving father. He had told me that all the plants were natives – many were 'cultivars' from Western Australia that had been grafted onto Victorian root stock. I had not entirely understood what he meant, but I nodded along politely as he waxed botanical. Bottle trees, desert daisies, grevilleas and banksias grew quietly amid carefully positioned boulders of Strathbogie granite. The colours, textures and aromas were distinctly Australian – a testament to life's possibilities and resilience.

Returning to the matter at hand, I began to explore which colours, textures and aromas were held in my glass.

'This one's darker than the other white wines we've tasted,' I remarked, turning the glass in my hand. 'I'd say it has a beeswax colour.'

Nodding in agreement, Matt instructed me to examine the surface of the wine. Mimicking his gesture, I held my glass to the light and tilted it slightly away from myself.

'You'll notice it has a copper tinge,' said Matt. 'That colour comes from the grape skin. The skins leave a blush of copper or pink in the wine. A lot of winemakers will then filter it aggressively to strip that colour away because the market seems to value pale white wines. But my feeling is that we should leave it alone and allow the wine to show its true colours.'

'Not that I'm an expert, but I think you're absolutely right,' I replied. 'What you're describing is something Japanese gardeners, poets and potters have known for centuries – so-called flaws can be their own source of beauty. Whereas Western culture has typically associated beauty with perfection and permanence, there's a long-standing tradition in Japanese culture of celebrating *im*perfection and *im*permanence. It's called "wabi-sabi".'

I ran my left hand over a dark, narrow groove in the grain of the hardwood table at which we were seated. 'In our regular world, something like this mark in the timber might be seen as a blemish, but from a wabi-sabi perspective it's appreciated because it's an expression of the natural order. This irregularity is a sign of the wood's history and changeability. What was once a seedling grew into a tree, which was then cut down and ultimately became this table. It's also a reminder that the wood will eventually age and decay, just like everything else. According to the wabi-sabi world view, marks like this don't detract from the table's aesthetic appeal – they enhance it.'

Matt clearly approved. 'This particular wood used to be part of the trellis system in the vineyard,' he said. 'It had been tossed aside and was rotting away on pallets. One day I realised that the timber was really good quality and we salvaged it to make the restaurant tables.'

'How wonderful. You made what someone else deemed worthless into something valuable and useful. You've also tied in the Japanese practice of "kintsugi", which is the art of fixing pottery. Instead of throwing a broken ceramic bowl or plate away, powdered gold is applied to join the pieces back together again. A ceramic repaired using kintsugi is often considered more precious because the golden lines of repair are unique to that object. They show the history of the object and the care with which it was restored.'

Matt gestured at the splash of gold in his glass. 'Which brings us back to pinot grigio. I don't see its colour as a flaw at all. If you drop the expectation that white wines should always be pale, you can see this wine has a beautiful colour. Just like those bowls that get fixed with gold, I think we should appreciate pinot grigio's colour as an important part of its story.'

'I bet you never realised you had such a wabi-sabi outlook!'

'I've learnt something new about myself,' he countered with a wink.

We proceeded to smell and sip. Notes of pear, peach and honey mingled in a summery music. As far as my palate was concerned, I might have been vacationing on a tropical island. It was quite the contrast to the chilly weather outside.

'Of all the wines we've tried so far, I think pinot grigio might be my favourite,' I remarked after several tastes.

'That's interesting. Why is that?' Matt was topping up our glasses as he spoke.

'I really enjoy that balance between roundness and freshness you were describing earlier. I also just like the flavour for no apparent reason.' I took a quick sip before holding my refilled glass up to the light to admire the colour once more. 'I think the other quality that makes me fond of pinot grigio is that it's a white wine grape with a pink skin. It's such a perfect metaphor for how appearances can be deceiving. But it goes further than that. The fact that some winemakers filter out any trace of the grape's skin colour is another perfect metaphor. Rather than accepting pinot grigio for what it is, people try to make it conform to *their* standards. That's something human beings do to each other all the time.'

'I guess you've had a bit of experience with that.'

'Well, yes, but I think it's something *everyone* has some experience of. You don't need to be a member of a marginalised group to have felt confined by other people's expectations. That was something I learnt from you a long time ago.'

Matt tilted his head curiously. I recalled our conversation on the bus ride back to Florence. I explained how, on first meeting, Matt seemed to tick all the boxes of social acceptability. 'I assumed you would naturally enjoy this ideal existence,' I said. 'But that just wasn't true. Of course, people *do* experience different degrees of hardship because of their social status. That's not the point. The point is that all of us have a lot more in common than we might think based on appearances. Our assumptions and stereotypes become major obstacles when it comes to connecting with other people.'

Matt concurred, with a story of his own. 'When I began my career in law, the firm flew all their new lawyers up to Sydney to have consultants teach us business etiquette. The consultants told us that it is only within the first few seconds of meeting someone that you form your enduring impression of them. Of course, that impression can change over time, but those initial moments have a much bigger impact than we might imagine. Knowing this, I try not to judge people, but of course it happens.'

'We *all* do it *all* the time,' I said. 'Categorising is something our brains do as an evolutionary mechanism to help make sense of the world and identify potential threats. No matter how hard we try, we'll likely always end up pigeonholing people. The main thing is to be aware of our judgements and to constantly question them. It's when we believe our judgements are the whole truth that we stop seeing people as people.'

As I spoke, I was thinking of an essay by the French philosopher Gabriel Marcel, titled 'The Spirit of Abstraction, as a Factor Making for War'. Marcel argued that 'abstraction' – the tendency to see particular groups of people as abstract entities – plays a pivotal role in making possible the atrocities of war. It is, after all, much easier to attack, enslave or kill a fellow human being when you view them as an 'idea' rather than a flesh-and-blood person. When we label someone an 'enemy' we no longer need to consider their thoughts, emotions, memories or aspirations. They become akin to an inanimate object, undeserving of our compassion or understanding. By abstracting away the common humanity of other people, we can justify doing terrible things.

'Of course, what you're saying applies to wine as well,' said Matt, gently turning his glass in his hand. 'People get so caught up in the labels and price points that they lose sight of the wine itself. For example, some wine aficionados might not want to admit that they like an eight-dollar bottle of wine because it doesn't fit their idea of a what a "quality" wine should be. But if you enjoy the wine, you enjoy the wine.'

'Learning to look at life without labels,' I said. 'It's something Eastern spiritual teachers talk about a lot. Our world can be so heavy with preconceived notions that we forget to appreciate the wonders right in front of us.' I pointed out the window at a small bottle tree outside. 'Just consider that tree. The word "tree" doesn't even begin to capture what *that* is. If you take the time to look at it with fresh eyes, without any labels at all, you can see that it's the most remarkable thing.'

We took a moment to contemplate the tree. It seemed such an innocent work of nature, yet any attempt to accurately capture what it was in my thoughts eluded me. Words were not enough.

'Life without labels,' Matt repeated warmly. 'It's something I get a real glimpse of when I'm spending time with my girls. They get so excited over the smallest things. Like you say, they have a sense of wonder because their minds aren't blocked by all these preconceptions.'

My eyes drifted from the bottle tree to a family walking in through the front entrance. There was a man and woman with a little boy. The man looked to be in his early thirties and was wearing a navy-blue yacht jacket, checked dress shirt and designer jeans. The woman looked a little younger and was dressed in a camel coat, black blouse, gingham skirt and brown leather boots. The little boy wore a red jumper and a sulky expression. The mother and father also looked annoyed. Maybe the parents had had a fight in the car on the way over and now the little boy was upset as well?

But wait, what was I doing? Not only did I have no way of knowing why any of them might be upset – I had no way of knowing if they were upset at all. Maybe they were grimacing because of the wind outside? I couldn't even know for certain whether the man and woman were a couple – perhaps they were brother and sister or even just friends? Who knew?

'What if we were able to see other people without any labels at all?' I asked, turning back to face Matt. 'I imagine even the most open-minded person would be surprised *and* horrified to realise how many prejudices they had.'

'I've certainly endeavoured to challenge my own prejudices over the years,' my friend confessed. 'It's funny you mentioned the Florence trip because it was such a great experience for me in terms of breaking down stereotypes. On that trip there were people from all kinds of backgrounds who had such different points of view to mine. Going to an all-boys private school, I had a social group that had been fairly narrowly defined up until then. Suddenly, I was forming friendships with people I would have never imagined getting along with. It was a real eye-opener.'

Matt glanced down at the table with a small smile. 'I remember becoming friends with you and loving how flamboyant you were,' he said.

'Of course I was flamboyant!' I replied with a chuckle. 'Our Florence trip was such an exciting time. But I have to admit the flamboyance was a bit of a performance. I didn't want people to see how insecure I was, so I overcompensated by being as camp and fabulous as possible. Although I feel much more comfortable with who I am nowadays, I still find myself lapsing into performance mode from time to time – particularly in awkward social situations. It's my rainbow-coloured armour.'

'Isn't that the best kind?'

I laughed. 'Armour's armour. It's really no different from guys who project a super macho self-image. I suppose we all have our ways of protecting ourselves. Of course, the problem with armour is that it's isolating. When you hide who you are to stop people judging you, you also stop them genuinely connecting with you.'

Matt nodded but didn't say anything. We both went quiet for a minute, silently sipping and gazing out the window.

'Do you ever feel isolated?' I asked.

'I was just thinking that,' he replied. 'Yes, I do sometimes. Being the CEO means shouldering a lot of responsibility and oftentimes making decisions that are unpopular with people without the full field of view. I often have to put my feelings to one side and pretend that things don't bother me, when in reality they do. It's true what they say – it can be lonely at the top.'

I did not tell Matt, but in that moment he reminded me of Queen Elizabeth I. Not in terms of dress sense or style – I could not quite picture him in thick white make-up, wearing a corset and neck ruff. What he did have in common with the 'Virgin Queen' was his sentiments about the loneliness of leadership.

This was something Elizabeth I felt acutely. We know this because she wrote poetry about it. The first stanza of her poem, 'On Monsieur's Departure', captures the feeling precisely:

> I grieve and dare not show my discontent,
> I love and yet am forced to seem to hate,
> I do, yet dare not say I ever meant,
> I seem stark mute but inwardly do prate.
> I am and not, I freeze and yet am burned,
> Since from myself another self I turned.

When I first read this, I was struck by the contrast between the depth of emotion conveyed in the poem and the regal, imperious, statue-like image I had garnered from Elizabeth's portraits. These paintings depicted a stony-faced ruler so heavily garbed in ornate gowns and jewels that she barely looked human. I had unthinkingly assumed that this was who she was. I had believed an 'abstraction'. Her poetry made me realise that beneath the iconic appearance and title, there was a woman with all too human thoughts and feelings.

'Listen to me carrying on!' Matt announced, shifting his voice to a jovial tenor. 'I know how fortunate we are. I have incredibly supportive parents and I'm surrounded by the most beautiful family. I also get to do my dream job in this amazing place, working with fantastic people. I have nothing to complain about.'

I took a long, pondering drink of pinot grigio.

'Funny thing is,' I remarked, 'I didn't think you were complaining. I thought you were being honest. There's no question that you've had your fair share of good fortune. I also know you work really hard and have sacrificed a lot to get where you are. On top of that, you're a human being, which means there are things you struggle with.'

He appeared uncomfortable and squirmed in his seat. 'If I'm honest, I don't like admitting to my struggles. It's not just about appearing ungrateful. It's also about showing weakness.'

I understood. 'It's ironic that people equate revealing their difficulties with weakness,' I said. 'In fact, it's one of the bravest things anyone can ever do.'

Matt looked puzzled. I couldn't blame him. For much of my life I had also believed that confessing my imperfections diminished me. It was a common misconception.

I continued: 'When we hide behind a facade of invulnerability, we're not really risking anything. We're shielded by the image that we're presenting to the world. We don't test our mettle by pretending to be something we're not. We demonstrate much greater fortitude when we front up as who we actually are, human frailties included. It's only when we're willing to shed our armour that our true strength of character is shown.'

'I've never thought of it like that.'

'I didn't think that way either until I read a book by social researcher Brené Brown, called *Rising Strong*. She writes about how courage and vulnerability are tied up together. There's a great line in that book: "Vulnerability is not weakness; it's our greatest measure of courage." I try to remember that whenever I feel scared to admit to a mistake or a failure.'

Matt was about to reply, but before he could open his mouth a flustered-looking man approached the table and launched into conversation. There was apparently an issue with a staff member that demanded Matt's immediate attention.

'Sorry mate,' Matt said, turning to me. 'I've got to deal with this. Would you be okay to wait here? I shouldn't be long.'

'Go, go, go,' I said, waving him away. 'I'll finish the bottle without you.'

'Do it!' he said, before rushing away.

Left alone at the table, I noticed that the man, woman and child I had seen earlier had taken a seat nearby. None of them looked annoyed anymore. They were all laughing, and the man was making silly faces to amuse the boy. I turned back to the tabletop and eyed the wabi-sabi mark in the grain.

'Who knows?' I whispered softly under my breath, and emptied my glass of wine.

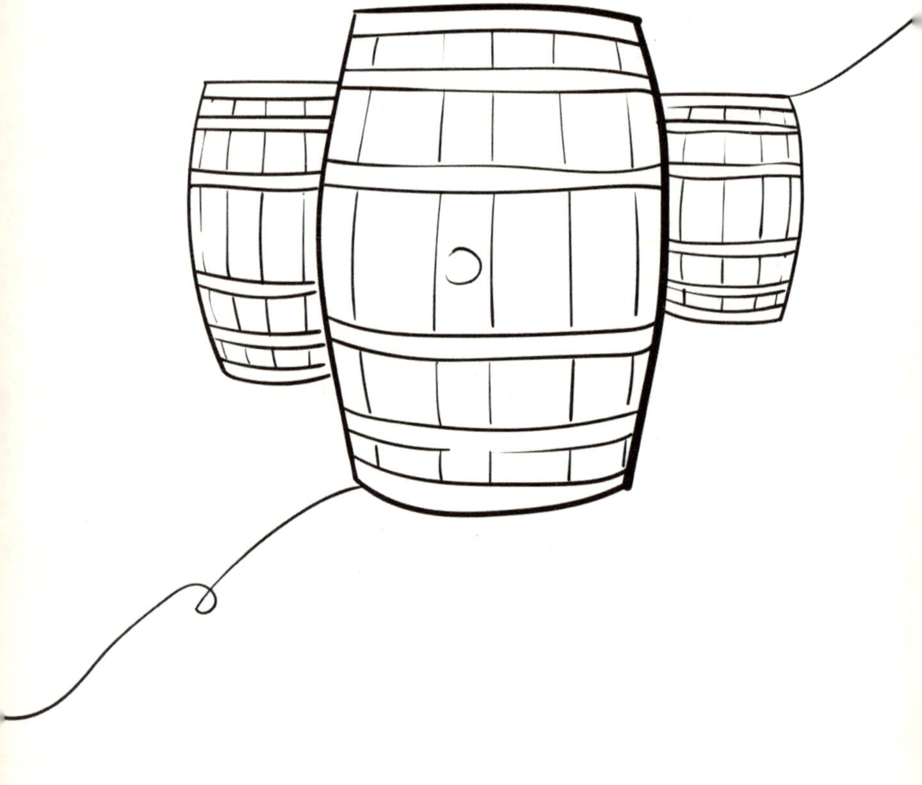

CHAPTER 8
Mourvedre

'You just need to remember the rule – always check up, down, across and in the square,' I said, gesturing with my pencil. 'That way you'll make sure you never double up a number by accident.'

Lilli nodded. 'What should I do next?'

'Now you've filled out most of this square, how about you see what you can find in the square above?'

'Okay,' Lilli replied, and focused intently on the square in question. 'Two can't go there, it can't go there, it can't go there, so it *has* to go there!' She confidently wrote down the number 'two' before turning to me with a satisfied smile.

'Perfect!' I gave her a thumbs up. 'Now I can see where the four goes in that square. Can you spot it?'

I hardly considered myself an expert, but my rudimentary knowledge of how to complete a sudoku puzzle was enough for Lilli to entrust me with her education. As she listened closely to my guidance, I was proud to watch my protégé progress.

We sat silently as Lilli filled in a 'four', 'seven' and 'nine'. She then turned to me with a look of profound seriousness.

'Why is there war?' she asked.

I had no idea where the question came from, but my time with Matt's daughters had taught me that it was best to go with the flow. I frowned as I considered how to answer. This was going to be a tough one. Couldn't we just stick with numbers?

'Well,' I began slowly, 'there are lots of reasons. The simple answer is that one group of people have a disagreement with another group of people and they believe that the best way to solve the conflict is by fighting.'

'But why can't they just fix the problem by talking?' It was an excellent question.

'Well ... sometimes people can't agree by talking, and that's when they decide war is the only option.' I was failing to mention that sometimes people did not even *try* talking, because they wanted to take over Europe, establish an Aryan master race and institute the rule of a 'thousand-year Reich'.

'War is stupid,' Lilli stated flatly, and returned to the puzzle.

I was tempted to explain that war was complicated and that to call it 'stupid' was perhaps an over-simplification. As an adult, I understood that war was an outcome of myriad sociological, political, cultural, ideological, economic, historical and psychological factors. Of course, I did not *like* war, I did not *agree* with war, I thought war was *appalling*. Nevertheless, I *accepted* war as an inevitable reality of our complex world.

It was easy to dismiss Lilli's remark as adorably naive. But was it, really? If I considered the definition of 'stupid', then the adjective applied perfectly to the practice of war. What could be less intelligent than human beings violently pitting themselves against each other in the name of conflict resolution? It was supremely primitive. Just because I was more 'educated' and 'mature' than Lilli, I had assumed I saw things more clearly. Perhaps the opposite was true? Lilli's mind was free from the various narratives used to explain and justify war. Perhaps she was the one with real insight.

'You're absolutely right,' I replied after a short pause. 'War *is* stupid.'

Matt walked into the room and gave a big smile. 'Looks like you guys are having fun!'

'We have a budding master on our hands,' I replied. 'We were just discussing war.'

Matt looked puzzled and then laughed.

'I like talking about the big questions of life with Pete too,' he said to Lilli. 'Can I borrow him for a bit?'

Lilli nodded amiably. Now she had the knack, she could happily complete the puzzle without any further help from her instructor.

As for me, it was time to taste some wine.

I had come to stay with Matt and his family for four days. I had a lull in work, and Mike was away visiting his family. It was an ideal opportunity to continue my wine education and enjoy a break from city life. As much as I had never considered myself a 'nature' person, my occasional visits to the Strathbogie Ranges had given me a new appreciation for time among the trees. I had discovered that my trips away from the urban sprawl brought refreshment and tranquillity. That said, I was not a complete convert. I could not yet see myself *ever* undertaking a camping expedition. The idea of voluntarily sleeping in a polyester shelter propped up with metal sticks, while going without access to a flushing toilet, was beyond my comprehension.

'I want to take you to the barrel hall,' Matt said as we drove away from his home.

'What are we drinking today?' I asked, secretly wondering how there could be any appeal to be found in a place called 'the barrel hall'.

'Mourvèdre,' he replied, 'also called "monastrell" or "mataro", depending on which country it's cultivated in. It's a red wine that's well grown in southern France and Spain, but not so much in Australia. The grape is late ripening and thrives in warmer climates. It's a comforting wine to drink on a cold winter's day.'

It *was* a cold winter's day – by Australian standards, at least. I was bundled up in several layers, my neck snuggly wrapped in a red Vivienne Westwood scarf. I could not have been happier. Any excuse to don a sweater, coat and scarf was a joyful occasion.

The car pulled up and I immediately started to question Matt's judgement. Why had he brought me to a monolithic warehouse? We were surrounded by acres of stunning countryside and there was a well-designed cellar door at our disposal – we had options! I exited the car and sombrely walked beside my friend, formulating a compelling argument for why it would be better to spend the afternoon in the cellar door restaurant, sharing a cheese platter.

We passed large metal vats and industrial-sized hoses. I was reminded of the sets used in the 1980s British science-fiction shows that Mike liked to watch. I could imagine the cast of *Blake's 7* or *Doctor Who* running about clad in questionable outfits using cheaply constructed plastic weapons to do battle with alien foes.

We approached a massive grey sliding door. It had a bright yellow 'Forklifts in Use' sign stuck to the front. 'What fresh hell is this?' I muttered under my breath. Matt passed through into a dark, cavernous room. I reluctantly followed.

Upon entering the barrel hall, all my cynicism melted away. Before I could get my bearings, I knew I was standing somewhere special. It was not entirely unlike walking through the grand wooden sanmon entrance gate of Nanzen-ji Temple in Kyoto. Of course, the barrel hall was not an exquisitely constructed example of 13th-century Japanese religious architecture. It was a huge concrete box, dimly lit and filled with towering metal racks holding rows of wooden wine barrels on their sides. Even so, the hall was permeated with a feeling of stillness and timelessness that I associated with sacred places. I half expected Mozart's *Requiem in D Minor* to begin playing in the background.

'I have to admit, I wasn't excited about coming here,' I confessed. 'But I get it now.'

'I knew you'd like it,' Matt said warmly.

I did not reply. I was busy absorbing my surroundings. The hall had a distinctly woody scent, mingled with what I could only describe as an 'alcohol sweetness'. It was a comforting smell, like the aroma of freshly baked bread or a lovingly laundered shirt.

'Most of what you see here are five-hundred-litre barrels,' said Matt, immediately adopting the role of tour guide. 'These barrels are nearly twice as large as the ones often used in Europe. The reason we use bigger barrels is to ensure gentler oak integration.'

I told my guide he was going to have dumb things down a little for me. 'What is oak integration?'

'It's how much the flavour of the oak from the barrel permeates the flavour of the wine. The fruit in our climate is subtler than warmer regions, so if we were to use smaller barrels, the oak elements would overpower the wine.'

'What does oak taste like?' I asked.

'Vanilla, cinnamon, toast, coconut.'

I recalled the hint of vanilla in Matt's chardonnay. That must have been oak.

'It can also give the wine an appealing smoky flavour, depending on the barrel's toasting level,' Matt said.

'Wow, you're going hard with the technical terms today. What is a toasting level?'

Matt chuckled. 'When a barrel's being made, to help bend the staves, the interior is often exposed to fire, thereby "toasting" the barrel. The level will vary depending on how heavily the barrel's been toasted. Different toasting levels impart different flavours into the wine. More heavily toasted barrels tend to impart flavours like smoke, spice and molasses.'

He pointed to one of the nearby barrels. 'If you look at this one for instance, you'll see its toasting level written on it.'

I examined the flat, circular top of the barrel facing out from its sideways position on the shelf. The words 'medium heavy toast' were carved into the wood in an elegant, capitalised font. Above this was inscribed a French name under which 'tonnellerie' was written. There was also a small, black sticker, which read 'fait par un artisan tonnelier'. Recalling my schoolboy French, I knew that 'fait par un artisan' translated to 'made by an artisan'.

'I guess "tonnelier" is French for "barrel maker"?' I said.

'That's right. The English word for "barrel maker" is "cooper", and the French word is "tonnelier". We use mainly French barrels made by several different coopers. You can see all their names written on the barrels.'

I began wandering through the shelves. I noted the names of the various tonneliers, written in distinctive fonts and often accompanied by a particular logo. I had no idea there was such a prolific number of barrel makers.

As I inspected the barrels from every which way, I discovered that many of them were stained with pink or red marks. This was evidently where red wine had managed to escape its oak confines. It looked as if the barrels were bruised or bleeding. The effect was not ugly, however. It was oddly beautiful.

'We have to periodically "top" the barrels with more wine because some evaporates over time,' Matt explained. 'They call the evaporated wine the "angel's share".'

The angel's share. I could not think of a better term. I loved the idea of invisible, benevolent entities floating over the barrels, growing joyfully tipsy on borrowed wine.

'Come with me,' said Matt. 'I want to show you something cool.' I followed him through the hall.

As we turned a corner, we were met with three enormous casks, many times larger than those filed away on the racks. These were also lying on their sides, so that their circular tops faced towards us. The tops were about two metres tall and reminded me of the round, wooden doors of the hobbit-holes in *The Lord of the Rings*.

'These barrels are 150 years old and made of English oak,' my friend announced.

'Wow,' I replied. It was humbling to think that these magnificent barrels had been made during the rule of Queen Victoria, by coopers who had long since left this world. The reverence I felt for the barrel hall continued to increase.

'Now let's drink some wine,' said Matt.

'I can smell vanilla,' I declared, imbibing a mouthful of purple-tinted mourvèdre. 'That must be the oak!'

Matt had set us up in metal chairs outside the barrel hall, facing rolling fields of wide, green countryside. It was a beautiful view, but the prevailing winds were chilly to say the least.

'Correct. I get vanilla, plum and pepper notes with this one. I'm interested to find out what you think of the flavour.'

'Do I sound insane or does this have a meaty flavour?' I asked.

'The first rule is that you *can't* be wrong. If you taste a meaty flavour, that's what you taste. And I know what you mean. It has a smoky bacon flavour.'

'Does the smoky quality mean it was matured in a barrel with a higher toasting level?'

'It sure does,' Matt replied.

I took another sip. It was a soft and supple red, friendly to taste.

'Tell me more about mourvèdre,' I requested.

'As I mentioned earlier, it goes by three different names, which is kind of fitting because this grape is a bit of a mystery.

Traditionally it has been used as part of blends rather than as a standalone variety. There's no general consensus on how to make it as a standalone variety or whether it even *should* be made as a standalone variety. Everyone seems to bring a different point of view to mourvèdre.'

I held my glass up against the broad, blue horizon and considered the wine's colour for a moment.

'Everyone seems to bring a different point of view,' I repeated. 'Isn't that what wine is all about?'

'How do you mean?'

'Well, this probably applies more to wine-tasting than winemaking, but one of the things I like best about wine is that it is unashamedly subjective.' I took a sip before continuing my thought. 'You've taught me that the point isn't to tick off a list of "correct" observations about the wine you're tasting. Rather, wine appreciation is the art of the individual taster exploring *their* experience to see what they can find.'

Matt smiled. 'I'm so glad you've picked up on that because it's a super important insight. Science tells us that no two people have exactly the same sense of smell and taste. If we did, something like deductive tasting would be easy. Everyone trying a particular vintage would just say "it tastes like strawberries" and be in complete agreement with one another. It doesn't work that way, and nor should it. Everyone's going to have their own understanding of the wine they're drinking, and that's a great thing.'

As if rehearsed, Matt and I paused the conversation to take a drink from our glasses. Any onlooker might have thought we were having an identical experience. We were both men of a similar height and age sitting in the same corner of the world, exposed to the same weather, sharing the same day, and drinking the same wine. But we were not having an identical experience. We never could.

I summoned the words of the author and critic Edmund Wilson: 'No two persons ever read the same book.'

'Of course,' I added, 'he didn't mean that literally. What he was saying was that no two individuals have ever read the same book in *the same way*. Obviously, this is also true in your world. No two persons ever drank the same wine.'

I cupped my glass in my hands, as if holding a mug of hot tea. It was an unconscious attempt to derive warmth from my beverage.

'It's not just differences in how our senses work that makes wine-tasting so subjective,' I continued. 'There are also differences in our memories, thoughts and feelings. You've taught me that drinking wine can be incredibly evocative, but what it evokes will vary depending on the taster's own life experiences. A wine can't remind you of a flower you've never smelt or a fruit you've never eaten or a place you've never visited.'

'Or, in your case, a book you've never read,' Matt replied with a grin.

The wind was beginning to pick up. I draped my scarf over my head to protect my ears from the cold. I must have resembled a Russian peasant woman. Matt glanced in my direction but did not bat an eyelid. He was well accustomed to my eccentricities.

'It's like the Heisenberg principle of wine,' I suggested, borrowing from Werner Heisenberg, the German physicist behind the uncertainty principle of mathematical inequalities. 'You can't divorce the wine observer from the wine being observed. Everyone's experience of wine is unique to them.'

'And that is precisely what frustrates me about all the elitist rubbish surrounding wine,' Matt said. 'People think they can't enjoy wine properly because they don't have the necessary expertise; that their experience will somehow be invalid.'

I could see the frustration in his face. Wine snobbery was a bugbear.

'Granted,' he said, 'a Master of Wine is better equipped to describe a wine's qualities or compare it with other vintages or tell where it was made without looking at the label. All the same, the enjoyment of a novice drinking a glass of fine wine is just as valid as the enjoyment of a wine expert. The novice will just have a different *kind* of experience from the expert. But as we've just discussed, *nobody* has exactly the same experience as anyone else, so it's a moot point.'

All at once, my scarf was whipped off my head by a strong gust of wind. It went flying in front of us, twirling on the air. Before I could think to chase it, Matt leapt from his chair and grabbed it.

'I think it might be time to retreat,' I said, as Matt handed me back the scarf. 'I don't dare risk losing any items of apparel.'

Matt laughed and suggested we head back into the barrel hall. I happily agreed.

'Have you ever heard of the Voynich manuscript?' I asked.

Matt shook his head.

'It's believed to have been written in the early fifteenth century, although the author is unknown. The manuscript is filled with strange illustrations of plants and astrological diagrams. Nobody knows what the illustrations mean because nobody can understand what the manuscript says. The text is written in code. Many people have attempted to crack the code, but without success.'

'How frustrating.'

I shrugged my shoulders. 'I'm sure it's hard for all those code breakers. But I'm glad we can't understand it. I hope they never translate the Voynich manuscript.'

'Why?'

My left hand was resting on a barrel. The surface was remarkably smooth, like a water-weathered pebble.

'We live in an age of disenchantment,' I replied. 'The scientific revolution has lifted the veil on so many things. The material world can be understood and explained with greater clarity than ever before. Not that this is a bad thing.

It goes without saying, science is essential. However ...'

Matt's phone rang. He tpulled it out, checked who was calling, looked back up at me and then returned it to his pocket.

'They can wait,' he said. 'You were saying?'

I wondered what pressing business he had put on hold in order to keep discussing an indecipherable Renaissance tome.

I picked up the thread again. 'I worry we lose something important when we reduce everything to quantifiable terms. What I love about the Voynich manuscript is that because we don't know what it means, it could mean *anything*. It might contain spells or erotic stories or instructions for building a time machine! But so long as we don't know, our imaginations have room to play. There's something magical about that, and I think we all need a little magic in our lives.'

'That's a wonderful thing about having young daughters,' said Matt warmly. 'There's no shortage of magic.'

I had seen his daughters at play, and he was not wrong. Enchantment was alive and well in Matt's home.

'There's no shortage of magic here either,' I countered, gesturing to the rows of barrels about us. 'It's why I mentioned the Voynich manuscript. I get that same sense of mystery looking at these barrels as I do when I look at illustrations from the manuscript.'

'I hate to disappoint you, mate,' Matt said with a wry smile, 'but we know what's inside the barrels.'

I laughed. 'I assumed you did. But from what you've told me, you never know for certain what the maturation process will deliver. There's an unseen alchemy going on inside these barrels. Who knows – there might be the best wine you've ever made resting in one of them?'

Resting. It was the correct word for the barrel hall. The whole point of the place was to give the wine time to transform through rest. The barrels also rested, silent and patient as they completed their task. Of course, their job was to do nothing at all. The barrels fulfilled their function by simply being.

'I certainly hope our best wine is in here somewhere,' my friend remarked. 'But you're right. We can never have complete confidence about how the finished product will taste. That's part of the fun. It's like opening a bottle of wine you've never drunk before. As familiar as you might be with a particular variety or winery or region, you can never really know how it's going to taste before it hits your palate.'

The idea appealed to me: the wine was an unknown quantity, but so was the taster.

'So, none of us can be sure what images might float through our mind when we smell or taste a glass of wine.'

Matt nodded in agreement. 'I've heard so many stories of people vacationing in Europe, having a wonderful time, and falling in love with a particular wine. They buy the wine in bulk, head back home, pull the cork on their first bottle and discover that the wine isn't as good as they remember. Of course, the wine itself hasn't changed – not enough time has passed. It's the circumstances that have changed. A bottle of Bordeaux can taste very different in a cramped London apartment compared to the gardens of the Château Lafite Rothschild.'

I imagined a British couple disappointedly downing their glasses of red, wondering what had gone wrong between their holiday and home. It was hard not to feel sorry for the hypothetical pair.

Matt's example reminded me of the quote by the ancient Greek philosopher Heraclitus: 'No man ever steps in the same river twice, for it's not the same river and he's not the same man.' Like wine, we go through our own maturation process.

'If we were to finish our bottle of mourvèdre a year from now,' I said, 'not only would the wine have changed. We would have changed as well.'

'You're messing with my head,' Matt joked as he reached for the bottle. 'But let's not wait a year to finish this off. I want the Matt and Pete we are today to enjoy it.'

He refilled our glasses, and we did just that.

Returning to Matt's home, I walked into the living room to discover Lilli still poring over her book of sudoku puzzles. She had finished the one that we had been working on and was attempting another.

'This one's much harder,' she told me. 'I'm stuck. Can you help?'

I took a seat next to her and began examining the puzzle. It was indeed more difficult, with considerably fewer numbers to work with. I checked every which way but could not find a single answer.

'I'm sorry, Lil,' I said. 'I don't know what to do. How about we have a break and come back to it?'

She agreed and we relocated to the sofa chairs near the fireside.

'Where's Dad?' she asked.

'He's off making phone calls for work. We've just been visiting the barrel hall.'

'I love the barrel hall,' she said.

'Me too.'

She turned to the fire and then looked back at me. The way she moved her head reminded me of her father.

'What were you and Dad talking about?'

Again, this was going to prove challenging.

'We were talking about how everyone sees things differently,' I replied after a beat. 'The way you see things is different to the way I see things and the way Dad sees things and the way Mum sees things. We were talking about how it's important to remember that.'

'Why?'

'Because each of us gets to experience the world in our

own way, which is kind of special when you think about it. Of all the people in the world who have ever lived or will ever live, only *you* get to know what it's like to be Lilli. Isn't that cool?'

She took a moment to consider the idea. 'And only *you* know what it's like to be Pete!' she pronounced.

'That's right!'

'What is it like to be Pete?'

This was a bridge too far. I was not even going to attempt a serious answer to such a precarious question.

'It's a lot of fun,' I replied with a smile. 'Especially when I get to do sudoku with you. Shall we try again?'

Lilli jumped from her seat, ran to grab the puzzle book and a pencil, and dashed back. She them both in my lap and returned to the chair beside me. She looked at me expectantly. The heat was on.

'Let's see what we can do,' I said, opening to the puzzle in question. It did not take more than ten seconds to spot where an eight belonged in the top-left-hand square.

'There we go!' I said, writing the number in its appointed spot. 'Now you have a turn.'

It was not long before Lilli had filled in two more numbers.

'I don't understand!' Lilli declared. 'We couldn't solve it before and now we can! What changed?'

'We did.'

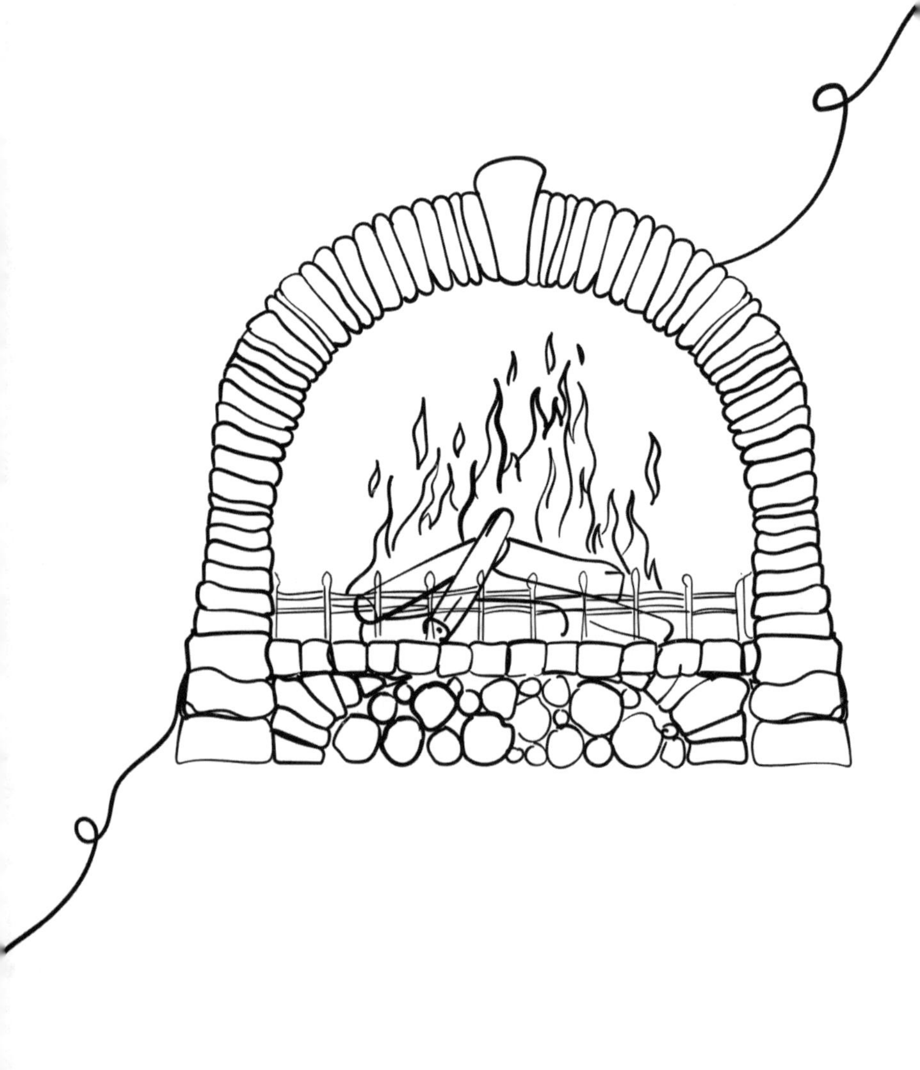

CHAPTER 9
Cabernet Sauvignon

'Why is cabernet called the king of the reds?' I asked.

Another day at the vineyard, another wine to learn about. I was making the most of my winter getaway. Matt and I were settled in front of the open fire in the lounge room. I was quite literally bundled up in a quilted blanket patched with burnt orange, saffron and clementine squares. Until this visit, I had never told Matt of my strong predilection for blankets, or how I amassed them around my home in anonymous piles that Mike referred to as 'nests'. When I had discovered the quilted blanket in the guest bedroom of Matt's house, I had proceeded to carry it around with me like Linus from the *Peanuts* comics. When Matt asked me why I was draped in a blanket like a Nepalese Sherpa, I was forced to confess my mild addiction to bedding.

Matt sat comfortably without a blanket in the armchair opposite. 'To answer your question, you need to know a bit about the Bordeaux region. It is basically a swamp. It's a really tough area to grow things, but wine grapes like the struggle.'

I was surprised by the description of Bordeaux as a 'swamp'. Although I'd never given it much thought, my mental picture of Bordeaux was of rolling, verdant hills. The word 'swamp' invoked Savannah blackwaters, alligator faces lazily resting on the waterline. But that was not what Matt meant. He was describing a cold, French swampland, mud clinging to the gumboots of the resident winemakers.

'Because of their thick skin,' he said, 'the cabernet berries were able to resist disease and ripen. Cabernet's ability to endure hardship made it perfect for that region. Cabernet also has small berries with intense colour and tannin. This makes it big and grippy and long-lived, giving it excellent ageing potential.'

His description of cabernet reminded me of Aretha Franklin. The lyrics of 'Respect' rang out in my head as Matt continued.

'The Bordeaux region has become famous for its cabernet-based blends. These wines command some of the highest prices in the world. They're widely considered the pinnacle of wines. Hence, cabernet became the king of reds.'

Matt picked up the bottle on the coffee table and poured two handsome glasses of home-grown cabernet. We said a quick 'cheers'.

After taking a few seconds to consider the colour, I remarked: 'It's a very, *very* deep red.'

'This is the benchmark on deep red,' Matt said. 'This is the deepest red.'

I took a long sniff of the wine.

'It's got a rich, intoxicating aroma,' I said. 'It reminds me of fruitcake.'

'"Richness" would normally describe ripeness in the fruit, so you might get fruitcake or ripe plum characters.'

Smelling my glass again, I remembered our tour of the barrel hall. 'There's also vanilla, which, as I learnt yesterday, means oak!'

'Spot on,' he confirmed. 'Oak is a little obvious in this wine right now. This vintage is only two years old, which is young for a cabernet. We've found cabernet knits together and matures in the bottle. Sometimes when you bottle cabernet quite young, the oak will show a little more than you might like. Over time, the oak tends to integrate.'

I took a measured sip. 'Wow. You can really feel the tannin.' When we began our lessons, a wine this tannic would have been too much for me to take. Evidently my palate had evolved.

'You sure can. This wine has both fruit- and oak-derived tannins, so it really doubles down on the tannin front.'

I took a more generous mouthful. 'Blackcurrant?'

'Spot on again! One of the famous descriptions with cabernet is "cassis", which is the French word for "blackcurrant".'

Like the mourvèdre we had shared the previous day, the wine had a warming quality. Unlike the day before, I was not relying on the warmth of the wine to compensate for extreme weather conditions. I much preferred this approach – a warming glass of wine in a warm room, beneath a warm blanket.

'This is perfect,' I said with a smile. 'This is fruitcake and a fireside. It reminds me of a Munich Christmas market.'

A few years earlier, Mike and I had travelled to Bavaria in Germany to visit a friend and his family. We had immediately fallen in love with Christmas in the northern hemisphere. Neither of us had ever been big fans of Christmas in Australia. Puddings with custard, and pine trees in the lounge room, always seemed a little out of place in stinking hot weather. The hanging lights, rich food and mulled wine of the festive season made so much more sense against a backdrop of darkness and snow.

'Wine has a great way of prescribing the setting in which it should be enjoyed,' Matt said. 'You're unlikely to drink this cabernet under a waterfall in Vanuatu – you're more likely to be reaching for a bottle of chardonnay. At a ski resort, you can leave the chardonnay in the fridge because you'd be looking for cabernet by the fire.'

'Absolutely,' I replied. 'Drinking this makes me imagine sitting in a library next to a pile of books.'

'Well, cabernet is definitely the right wine for a reader,' said Matt. 'If you were going to label any wine the philosopher's wine, I think it would be cabernet.'

I could hear the chiming voices of Matt's daughters in the background, getting ready for bed. The fire crackled and shifted. Burning amber, blue and black shards of wood collapsed as they yielded to the heat.

'How long does cabernet take to peak?' I asked.

'Well, it depends. Cabernet from warmer climates tends to develop faster. Then from regions like Bordeaux, cabernet might take fifty years to peak.'

Fifty years struck me as an extravagantly long period of time. 'Have *you* ever drunk a fifty-year-old bottle of cabernet?'

'I've had a 1929 Château Pontet-Canet,' he replied. 'It was mind-numbingly good. That was in 2007.'

The mathematics ran through my head. 'You drank a *seventy-eight-year-old* bottle of wine? That wine survived the Second World War!'

'Right? We're super lucky the Nazis didn't get to it!'

Lucky indeed. I could only imagine the price tag on such a precious commodity. 'What was the occasion?'

'It was on the Bordeaux trip I went on with Dad. We had it at Maxim's, the famous restaurant in Paris. It was an amazing, beautiful life memory.'

There was a brief lull. I imagined Matt and his father seated in this hallowed eatery, amid the murmuring traffic of patrons and waitstaff, surrounded by art nouveau decor. I pictured the perfectly pressed French waiter decanting the bottle; the delight, the anticipation, the sight, the smell, the first taste. Seventy-eight years of waiting for that singular moment in time.

'This is very young to be drinking cabernet,' Matt said, gently breaking the silence. 'We would normally hold our cabernet back for a couple of years before releasing to the market. With cabernet, you're often rewarded for cellaring. Cabernet likes time.'

I heard a door open behind us and turned to see Lilli dressed in her pyjamas. She gave her father a hug. She then turned around and, to my surprise, gave me a hug too.

'Goodnight Pete,' she said.

'Goodnight Lilli,' I replied.

She left the room, and we returned our attention to the wine.

'It's funny to hear you talk about the value of ageing,' I remarked. 'Nowadays, we live in a youth culture. People associate age with weakness and decline. It's uncommon for people to discuss ageing in a positive sense.'

'That's true. Back in the day, elders were revered as an invaluable source of knowledge. These days, we seem quick to shuffle off our elderly into nursing homes. Why do you think that's the case?'

I considered the question. 'I think it's tied up with our modern ideas of success. The contemporary view of life is that it's a journey from A to B. The whole point is to "get it right" – get the partner, the children, the career, the house, the best body – the list goes on. We believe that once we've ticked all those boxes, we'll hit this magical plateau called happiness.'

I took a sip, pausing to think.

'But, of course, that's not the way it goes,' I said. 'We're constantly going through ups and downs, learning new things and making mistakes. We *never* reach a place where all our troubles disappear. Ageing reveals this more than anything else. Old age, sickness and death are universal truths. The dream of success we've been sold is a lie, and that's a hard pill to swallow.'

I had borrowed the words 'old age, sickness and death' from the teachings of Buddhism. It was said that before the Buddha became a spiritual seeker, he was a wealthy prince named Siddhartha Gautama. He was raised in a life of pleasure and privilege, shuttered away from the hardships of the world. Then one day, he went on an outing to see beyond the palace walls. On this trip he was confronted with the sight of an elderly man, a sick man, and a corpse. Deeply moved by these inevitable realities of life, he chose to renounce his royal robes in exchange for those of a wandering monk. Later, sitting beneath the branches of the Bodhi Tree, the sacred fig, Siddhartha Gautama is said to have achieved enlightenment. He became the Buddha.

Sitting amid my own version of spiritual bliss, I returned to the topic of passing time. 'The problem is that we don't give ageing the credit it deserves. For my part, getting older has brought so much more contentment into life. Over the years I have learnt to relax into myself and not be in such a rush to get to the *next* thing. I take more time to savour each day as it comes.'

As if in Pavlovian response to the word 'savour', we both drank from our glasses. The vanilla aroma of the wine made a lovely counterpoint to the woody, charcoal smell of the open fire.

'Growing and making cabernet is all about slowing down and learning to enjoy the journey,' said Matt. 'The sunlight that hit the buds this year will help form the grapes next year, which will become the fruit that will go into the winery, that will probably be matured for two years, then it will be bottled and cellared for two years. That's *five* years at that point, before we get to send it to market. In business terms, that's a cashflow nightmare. But cabernet is one of the most beautiful and complex varieties. It's totally worth the wait.'

Werner Herzog, a famous German film director, directed a documentary which explored the Chauvet-Pont-d'Arc Cave, in the south of France. The cave served as a canvas for prehistoric paintings dating back 32,000 years. Bison, lions, leopards, hyenas, bears, deer, horses and even rhinoceroses inhabit its limestone walls. Through radiocarbon dating, scientists have been able to determine that certain paintings were left unfinished by one ancient artist, only to be completed by another some *five thousand years* later. In an era where the minute-long delay of an app download can feel unbearable, the thought of an artwork being completed over millennia is incomprehensible ... but awe-inspiring.

'There's another thing,' Matt said. 'You can drink cabernet in its youth, like we are right now, and enjoy all its youthful qualities. Then in five years it will be very different, but still great to drink. Then ten, fifteen, twenty years from now it will be the same story – different but delicious. Then you have my example of drinking a wine that was seventy-eight years old, which was just remarkable. It wasn't fresh and fruity. It had all these wonderful secondary and tertiary characteristics, but was still very much alive. Cabernet delivers so much that's new, each and every time. It's amazing.'

'So, there's no "wrong" stage to drink it,' I mused. 'The characteristics simply evolve. Just like people! Whether we're children, teens, adults or elderly, there's so much to appreciate at every stage in life.'

As soon as I said this, I felt like a fraud. Although I believed what I was saying, I wasn't speaking from experience. My own relationship with the 'earlier' versions of myself was more fraught than appreciative.

'I *say* that,' I confessed, 'but when I reflect back on who I was when we met all those years ago, I can't help feeling a little ashamed.'

'Why?' Matt seemed genuinely taken aback. This surprised me. I assumed it was obvious. For me, the person Matt had met in Italy was deeply insecure, overly sensitive, self-involved and awkward. By turns wildly flamboyant and darkly melancholic, I was, by my own estimation, a total handful. Had he met someone different?

'When we first met, I was struggling with my sexuality

and my relationship with my parents,' I explained. 'I was depressed and anxious. I often behaved in ways I'm not proud of. I sometimes wish I could go back and do it all over again.'

My friend tilted his head at my words. 'It makes me sad that you want to throw away who you were back then,' he said. 'Of course, everyone sees their own "imperfections" in a much stronger light than others. I look at you and think, you were great then and you're great now. Of course, you seem a lot happier now, which is fantastic. I know you were going through a lot back then, but it didn't make you any less of an enjoyable human to be around.'

I smiled and rearranged my blanket and cushions for greater comfort. 'Thank you for saying so. It's probably something I can learn from cabernet – to appreciate those earlier stages for what they were. Nineteen-year-old Pete was just doing his best with what he had to work with at the time. You loved him, so why can't I?'

It was a sentiment expressed by the often misunderstood German philosopher Friedrich Nietzsche. Between discussing the death of God and the rise of the Übermensch, Nietzsche had praised the virtue of wholly embracing life – past, present and future. He had used the Latin term 'amor fati': the love of fate. In his book *Ecce Homo,* he wrote: 'My formula for human greatness is amor fati: that one wants nothing to be different, not in the future, not in the past, not for all eternity.' I made a mental note to peruse my copy of Nietzsche's *The Gay Science* (later retitled *The Joyful Wisdom*) when I got home. I enjoyed reading it on public transport for the quizzical looks it evoked from fellow passengers.

'You talked earlier about "relaxing into" yourself,' Matt recalled. 'That is something people often say about cabernet. It needs time to relax. What's physically happening is the tannin is binding together in long polymer chains, so it doesn't feel as grippy, harsh or drying anymore. You see, tannin is bitter and in high concentration is registered by the body as poison. The more time you leave the cabernet, the more time the "poison" has to drop away. In the process, the wine becomes silky and smooth.'

'Aha!' I exclaimed. 'Cabernet provides another great metaphor. We all have a choice about what to do with the poison we experience in life – all the hurt feelings, failures and disappointments. We can hold onto them, becoming more bitter and resentful in the process. Or we can choose to forgive and move on. Cabernet is an amazing example of what happens when you release the poison. You become more delightful as you mature.'

I remembered watching an interview with the psychologist and Holocaust survivor Edith Eger after I had finished reading her book *The Choice*. Here was someone who had experienced unimaginable horrors and trauma. After her mother was murdered in the gas chambers at Auschwitz, Edith was relocated to another concentration camp where she was forced to eat grass to survive. Before being rescued by US soldiers in 1945, she had grown so weak and malnourished that she was left for dead. This was someone who had every reason in the world to be filled with anger. But she was not. In the interview, I saw a woman radiant with kindness, compassion and good humour. Instead of harbouring resentment, she had dedicated her life to supporting other people through *their* struggles. Letting go of poison was a powerful thing.

There was a lesson there for us all. For a winemaker like Matt, it was also a reassurance – trust yourself, and trust in time. 'One thing winemaking has reminded me is that it's the process, not the outcome, that matters most,' he said. 'You make all these decisions about how to grow the grapes, when exactly to harvest, and throughout the winemaking process. Of course, you're going to make mistakes, but you can correct them. You can readjust. The key thing is completing each stage to the best of your ability. So long as you remain focused on the quality of the process, then that will consistently reveal itself in the quality of the wine. When you've got such a long time frame to work with, you really can't think about the outcome. Whether the wine's going to be drunk ten or fifty years from now, the detail in the moment is what really counts. Ultimately, you don't know when the wine is going to be drunk, so the outcome becomes irrelevant.'

I had never considered it before, but the essential factor of *when* a wine is drunk was almost always outside the winemaker's control. This felt especially true with a wine like cabernet, which might be cellared for years or decades at a time. Had the creators of Matt's bottle of 1929 Châteaux Pontet-Canet contemplated its possible future? At the time of bottling, jazz was considered a radical innovation in the French music scene. Who among them could have anticipated their wine being enjoyed almost eighty years later, in the same year that Beyoncé and Shakira's 'Beautiful Liar' topped the French charts?

It got me wondering whether Matt had imagined a bottle of his own wine being dusted off and opened in fifty, or even eighty, years' time.

'To be honest, I haven't spent a lot of time thinking about it,' he said. 'I think more about the kind of occasions where it might be enjoyed. I love that the wine I make can bring people together. At what point in the future that ends up happening, I really don't mind. But the thought that we could make something of such a high quality that it could endure, potentially beyond my own lifetime ... Well, *that* is a beautiful thing.'

'It really is such an amazing legacy to leave,' I said. 'Along with your children, of course!'

I couldn't forget Matt's daughters. As someone who rarely spent time with children, I was surprised to discover how much fun was to be had. Whether it was helping Lilli with a puzzle, looking at Mathilda's drawings or playing peekaboo with Ella, there was always an abundance of laughter and joyful noise. While I remained happily childless, I had decided that having children was perhaps not so burdensome after all.

'Imagine my children enjoying a wine that I've made, after I'm gone,' Matt said. 'It's such a lovely thought.'

'Imagine your *grandchildren* enjoying a wine that you've made!'

'Crazy!' he said, laughing. 'That's a long way off, Pete. That's maturity on a whole different level.'

I laughed along with him. A crazy thought indeed, and one that must have seemed so far off in 1929 to those vintners in Bordeaux. I wondered if any of their grandchildren had enjoyed the fruits of their labour, and what it must have been like for them. Would they have taken time to consider their grandparents' love or cares or hopes for the future? I hoped so.

With our cabernet all but gone, poor Matt was looking weary. Over the past two days I had seen him deal with phone calls with lawyers, dramas among staff, unfulfilled deliveries, inclement weather – all the clamour of running a vineyard and cellar door. Just witnessing his day-to-day life made me want to lie down.

I took one last taste from my glass and put it aside. Matt yawned, cheerful but tired. Our bottle was empty, and the evening was ending. The fire was mellowing, quiet embers giving an aura of cosy stillness. A perfect finish to the day.

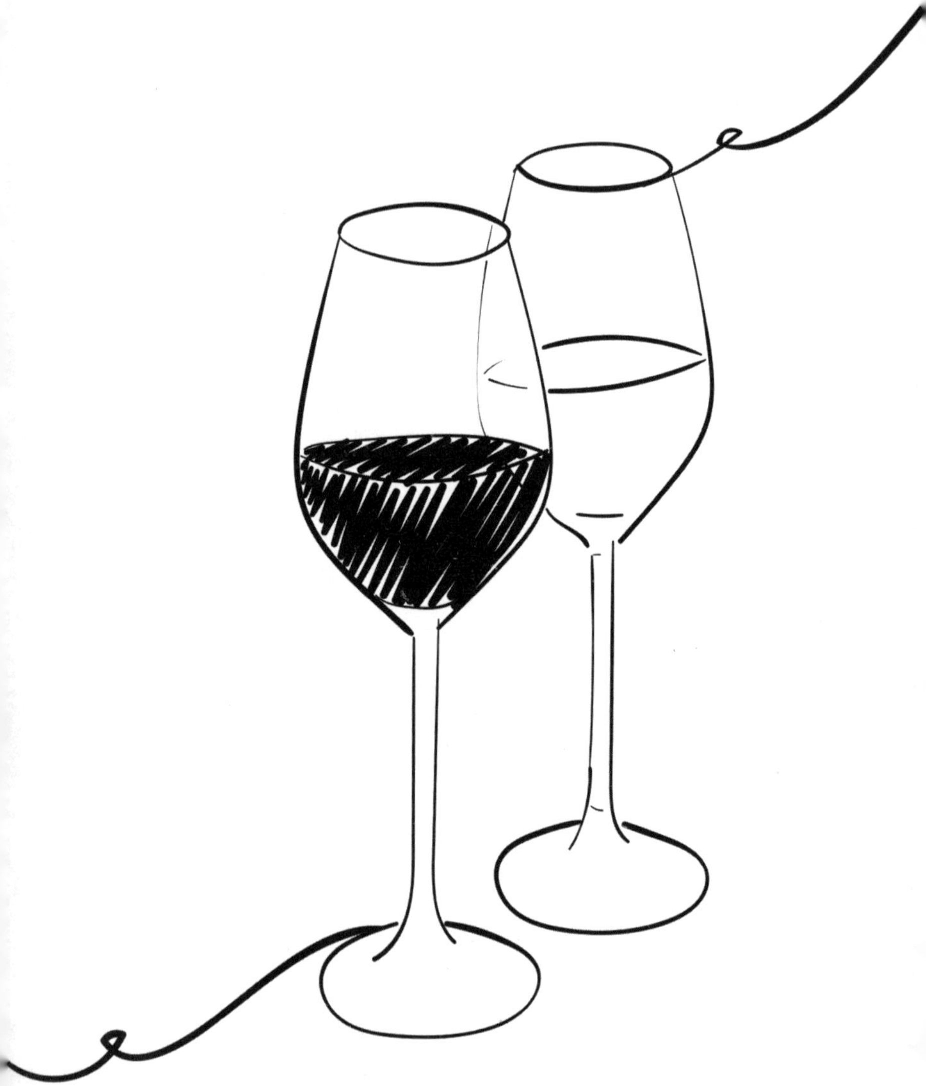

CHAPTER 10
Merlot

Heavy droplets hit the windows of Matt's office. It was reassuring to witness a downpour from the vantage of a safe, warm room. I closed my eyes, listening to the tides of rain strike the rooftop. There was a peculiar rhythm to it as it ebbed and flowed at unpredictable intervals. I recalled a Zen proverb: 'The sound of rain needs no translation.'

I opened my eyes to see Matt pouring our wine. He had originally intended to take the afternoon off to spend time with me before I headed home later that evening. But plans had changed. Pressing business demanded his attention. He had gone to the office first thing in the morning and I had not expected to see him again before I left. My revised strategy had been to spend the afternoon grazing on food and reading my book at the cellar door.

Lost in the pages of Patti Smith's *Just Kids*, mindlessly consuming a bowl of hand-cut chips, I almost failed to notice that my phone was ringing.

'Come on over to the office, mate,' he had said when he rang. 'Let's fit one more red in before you leave.'

'Are you sure you have the time?'

'I'll make the time.'

As I crossed the open area between the cellar door and the head office, a smattering of heralding raindrops had hit my head. The clouds rumbled and the air was thick with the musky scent of coming rain.

It was just as I had stepped into the office that the heavens unleashed. Perfect timing.

So it was that I found myself sharing an unexpected bottle of merlot with Matt as the rain came down.

Matt had, somehow, found room among the stacks of paper on his desk to fit our glasses. A friend had recently told me about *The Life-Changing Magic of Tidying Up* by Marie Kondo. The gist of the book was that a person should only keep possessions that 'spark joy', and throw everything else away. While I was dubious of claims that tidying could be 'life-changing', I was tempted to ask Matt if his desk clutter 'sparked joy'. I decided not to.

'Genetically speaking, merlot is a cousin of cabernet,' Matt said as he finished charging our glasses. 'Cabernet and merlot share a number of common traits. The vines have similar shaped leaves and berries. However, where cabernet has small berries and lots of tannin, merlot has bigger berries and much less tannin. This makes merlot a softer and more velvety variety.'

I examined the wine's colour. Like shiraz and mourvèdre, this wine had a purple tinge to it. Matt informed me that it would gradually shift to red. It had not occurred to me that just like its aromas and flavours, the colour of wine also changed with the passage of time. Of course, this made perfect sense. A bottle of wine was not a static thing.

'In the industry we call merlot "cabernet without the pain" because it's so much softer to drink,' said Matt. 'That's part of the reason Bordeaux winemakers often use merlot as a blending wine with cabernet. It softens the cabernet and makes it more approachable.'

'This smells sweet,' I said, distracted by the aroma. From the moment Matt had opened the bottle, the wine's perfume had piqued my interest. It was delicious, and difficult to ignore.

'I know what you mean, but technically "sweet" isn't a smell. How else might you describe it?'

I moved my nose close to the rim of my glass. Hints of cherry, blackberry and plums floated on the air. But its fragrance reminded me of something more specific.

'Ripe banana ... pastry ... toffee ... vanilla ... cinnamon ... banoffee pie!'

'I love that description!' Matt affirmed. 'As you know, a lot of those characteristics come from oak. Something that sets this wine apart from the others we've tasted is that it was aged in one hundred per cent American oak. As you would also remember, we mainly use French oak barrels.'

'What's the difference?'

'The difference between French and American oak is a

little like the stereotypical difference between French and American people. In simple terms, French oak is generally more restrained, while American oak is typically more boisterous. Both are good – just different!'

Describing a variety of wood as 'restrained' or 'boisterous' was something I never would have considered before beginning my lessons with Matt.

We took our first sips. 'I can see what you mean about it being soft and velvety,' I said. 'This is so easy to drink.'

'It's much less structured than cabernet,' Matt said. 'It's relaxed and comfortable. It's you wrapped up in your blankets, Pete!'

I chuckled and took another sip. 'It's doesn't ask too much of the drinker. It's gentle. I'm a fan.'

It was clear that Matt was too. 'Merlot often gets a bad rap from winemakers because they tend to prize structured wines,' he said. 'But I love that merlot is soft and undemanding. And yet, it's *because* of those qualities that it's sometimes frowned upon.'

Without warning, my mind grew filled with unpleasant memories. Schoolyard taunts of 'faggot', 'poofter' and 'homo' came rushing back. As a pudgy, camp teenager who loved reading and loathed sports, I was considered 'soft' in every negative sense of the word. As far as many of my fellow students were concerned, I was beneath contempt. My 'softness' made me the object of ridicule. I shook the memories aside, but their message remained with me.

'Softness isn't prized much in people either,' I pointed out. 'We're much more likely to praise someone for being tough or strong. All too often, qualities like gentleness or kindness are equated with weakness.'

'Sad but true,' Matt replied. 'You know, my grandfather on my mother's side was one of the most kind and gentle men I've ever met. Looking back, I wish I had spent more time with him. When I was young, I was much more preoccupied with kicking around a football than having a conversation with him. He was such an unassuming man – he tended to fade into the background for me. I didn't really learn to appreciate what a remarkable person he was until later in life.'

I could hear the regret in my friend's voice. I was about to say something comforting about how it's easy to criticise yourself in hindsight, but I noticed he was deep in thought. I remained silent and waited for him to speak.

'Remember that day in the vineyard when we were talking about how wine relies on humanity and humanity relies on wine?' he asked.

'Absolutely.'

'Well, the same is true of kindness. It's not a one-way transaction. Both the receiver of kindness *and* the giver of kindness benefit from it. It's reciprocal. That's the thing people seem to forget. Kindness is good for everyone!'

This statement seemed to come from left field, as if Matt were debating with someone who was not in the room.

Naturally, I agreed with him. I wondered if he realised that he was also echoing the words of Shakespeare: 'The quality of mercy is not strained. It droppeth as the gentle rain from heaven upon the place beneath. It is twice blessed: it blesseth him that gives and him that takes.'

But it wasn't just the Bard that Matt's words conjured. 'What you're describing is something the Buddha taught,' I said. 'He instructed his followers to cultivate loving kindness for their own wellbeing. He described eleven benefits of possessing a kind heart, including serenity, untroubled sleep and protection from harm. He also said that loving kindness gives your face a radiant glow. That one is hands down my favourite. It makes me so happy to know that even the Buddha was concerned with good skincare!'

As Matt laughed I went to take another sip, only to discover that my glass was empty. I had quaffed the lot without even noticing. I felt flushed and warm and ready to drink more. I reached over, topped up Matt's glass, and refilled my own.

As I began my second round, I realised that in our eagerness to discuss the wine's smooth and easy qualities, we had failed to mention any of its flavours. I could taste ripe plum and black cherry. There were also hints of coffee and chocolate.

'I'll have to tell Lu that kindness is good for her skin!' said Matt. 'Not that she needs to know. Lu is incredibly kind. In fact, I credit her with teaching me the value of kindness.'

In a sudden shift, the rain picked up speed. It hammered on the roof so loudly that Matt and I stopped speaking. We stared out the windows. Matt's office offered a panoramic view of water showering from every angle. I was reminded of going through a car wash.

'The power of Mother Nature,' Matt observed. My memory sparked. I put down my glass and reached into my backpack. After fumbling around, I pulled out a small, brown cardboard box. I handed it across the desk to my friend.

'What's this?' he asked.

'Open it,' I said.

After gently untucking the cardboard tag, Matt reached into the box to remove an eight-inch-tall carving of an ancient Greek goddess.

'It's Demeter,' I explained, 'the Olympian goddess of agriculture and fertility of the Earth.'

The statuette depicted Demeter seated on a throne, dressed in classical robes. In her right hand she held aloft a flaming torch, which she used to seek out her daughter Persephone in the underworld. In her left hand she grasped a bundle of wheat, symbolising the harvest. Curled up at her feet was a tiny piglet – an animal often sacrificed in honour of the goddess.

'It's just a small thank-you present for having me,' I said. 'As you're such a devotee of Mother Nature, I thought you needed a statue of her for your office.'

Matt placed the figure in front of him. 'Thank you so much, mate. I love it. That's super kind of you.' He got out of his chair, walked over, and gave me a hug.

'You're welcome,' I said as he returned to his seat. 'Speaking of kindness, you were talking about Lu?'

He did not reply immediately. He was looking intently at the statuette, turning it around to view it from various angles.

Eventually, he looked back up at me. 'Before Lu and I got together, kindness wasn't something I put much stock in. Then I fell in love with her and everything changed. She opened me up. She showed me the importance of gentleness and affection, just by being who she was.'

I was amazed by the influence that a good example could have. In my experience, simply instructing someone how to be rarely achieved the desired outcome. It was usually only when a person was *shown* a different approach to life that lasting change occurred. Lu had not taught Matt kindness by telling him to be kind. She had taught him kindness by *being* kind. This was something people so often missed in their eagerness to offer advice. I was as guilty of this as anyone. I frequently reminded myself of the wise words of the Brazilian author Paulo Coelho: 'The world is changed by your example, not by your opinion.'

'Why don't we value kindness more?' Matt asked. Good question.

I studied my wine through the top of my glass. 'You're no doubt familiar with the Taoist concept of yin and yang?'

'Sure. Good and bad, black and white, light and dark.'

'Exactly so. Yin is the "negative" principle associated with passivity, receptivity, gentleness, darkness, coolness, and water. Yang is the "positive" principle associated with activity, power, dominance, light, heat, and fire. Although the two principles appear separate, Taoism teaches that they're opposite ends of the same spectrum. You can't have one without the other. The essential idea of yin and yang is one of balance.'

I took a small sip. I was attempting to make my second glass last longer than the first.

'We're living in a yang-oriented society,' I continued. 'Think of all the qualities our culture encourages – growth, busy-ness, winning, wealth, passion, production. These are all yang characteristics. Attributes like restfulness, stillness, gentleness and kindness belong to yin.'

'And we look down on yin thanks to our preference for yang,' Matt sighed.

'Correct. Yin has been out of fashion for a while now. We're hopelessly out of balance, and feeling the effects. You only need to look at the high incidences of burnout and stress-related illness to see that. People are sorely lacking yin.'

This was a slightly pointed remark. From what I could tell, Matt lived an exceedingly yang lifestyle – always going, going, going. However, if Matt realised my comment was in part directed towards him, he did not let on.

'Perhaps this yang focus is also why some people look down on merlot?' my friend pondered. 'From the way you describe yin and yang, I would say that merlot is a yin wine.'

Soft and relaxed. It was true – merlot possessed quintessentially yin characteristics. I had no gauge of how the principles of yin and yang influenced the thinking of winemakers, but it was a working hypothesis.

'Perhaps,' I replied.

'Doesn't yin and yang also describe the differences between men and women?' Matt asked. It was interesting that this ancient Chinese concept, popularised in the third century BCE by the philosopher Zou Yan, was so widely understood in the modern world.

I nodded. 'According to Taoist philosophy, yin is feminine, and yang is masculine – which makes sense when you think of traditional gender roles. Needless to say, the idea that men are naturally hard and dominant while women are naturally soft and receptive is extremely old-fashioned.'

'It might be old-fashioned, but we still carry those ideas of gender with us,' Matt said. 'Growing up, I thought that manhood was all about being tough and never letting your guard down. It took me a long time to realise that as a man I could be both strong *and* gentle.'

Pulling my phone out of my pocket, I quickly typed until I found the image I was after. It was the taijitu – the symbol of 'yin' and 'yang' as a circle divided by an S-shaped line into equal black and white segments. Within the black half was a small white circle, and within the white half was a small black circle.

Holding up my phone to show Matt, I pointed to the symbol on the screen. 'What you're describing is exactly what the concept of yin and yang is all about,' I said. 'The taijitu symbol shows that yin and yang not only complement each other – they *contain* each other. There is yin in yang and yang in yin.'

I put away my phone and picked up my glass. 'It was the ancient Roman playwright Terence – who also happened to be a freed African slave – who said: "I am a human being: nothing human can be alien to me." Regardless of our gender or sexuality or race or anything else, each one of us can be cruel or kind, domineering or submissive, judgemental or compassionate. How we show up in the world depends on which qualities we nurture in ourselves, and which ones we don't.'

I explained that the Vietnamese Buddhist Master Thích Nhất Hạnh used the analogy of watering a garden to illustrate this point. He described the mind as a field containing seeds of every quality a human being could possess. There are seeds of happiness and understanding, and seeds of fear and jealousy. The garden of your mind will grow depending on which seeds you water. If you wish to have joy in your life, you must water the seeds of joy. If you water the seeds of hatred, then hatred is what you will get.

'Upon reflection,' said Matt, 'I see that's one of the big reasons I left the corporate world. It was difficult for kindness to grow in that environment – it was virtually forbidden. As brutal as working with nature can be, it's a much kinder world than the one I left behind.'

The room had grown quieter. The rain had slowed to a drizzle. Glimpses of sunlight and blue sky were beginning to show through the veil of dark grey clouds.

'In Zen Buddhism, they talk about "Buddha-nature",' I said. 'It's the idea that all beings, right down to the tiniest insect, are intrinsically enlightened. This means that *everyone* is fundamentally good and wise. The reason that we are sometimes unkind or foolish isn't because we've somehow lost our Buddha-nature. Rather, we've lost our *awareness* of it.'

I pointed out the window towards a small patch of clear sky where the sun was shining through. 'The metaphor they use is of clouds covering the sky. The clouds represent all the confusion and suffering that covers up our true nature. But the fact that the sun is hidden behind clouds doesn't mean it's not there. It just means we can't see it.'

Gazing at the ray of sunshine, Matt took a thoughtful mouthful of merlot. 'It's kind of the opposite to the idea of original sin,' he said.

'Yes, I suppose you could describe Buddha-nature as "original goodness".'

The downpour had entirely stopped. An aura of stillness prevailed. The world seemed so peaceful without the ruckus of the rain.

'Knock, knock.' It was Luise, standing in the office doorway. I could tell that somewhere along her journey to the office she had not been lucky enough to avoid the rain. Her normally bright blonde hair was dark and wet.

'I was looking for Pete,' she said cheerfully, before turning to me. 'Mathilda wanted me to give you this drawing. It got a little bit damp, but it should be fine.'

She handed me a sheet of paper, illustrated with several dramatically colourful stick figures. Although it was difficult to make out, I assumed this was a family portrait.

Leaning over my shoulder, Lu pointed to one of the taller stick figures. 'Mathilda told me to tell you that this one's "sweet Pete".'

Mathilda had used pink and blue pencils in her rendering of me.

'I love how skinny I look!' I exclaimed. 'Thank Mathilda very much from me. I love it. It will have pride of place on our refrigerator. Tell her that her artwork reminds me of Paul Klee.'

Both Matt and Lu laughed. 'I'll be sure to pass that on,' said Lu with a wink. 'Okay, I'll leave you guys to it.'

'We should probably finish up anyway,' I said. 'Matt, I should let you get back to work.'

He nodded and let out a sigh. 'I'd rather hang out and

discuss Zen Buddhism, but I have to get this stuff done.'

I finished my last share of merlot and placed my empty glass on the desk.

'Thanks so much again for the statuette, mate,' said Matt, walking over to give me another hug.

'Don't mention it,' I replied, returning my friend's embrace. 'Thank *you* so much for all your hospitality and making the time for me today.'

'It was my pleasure.'

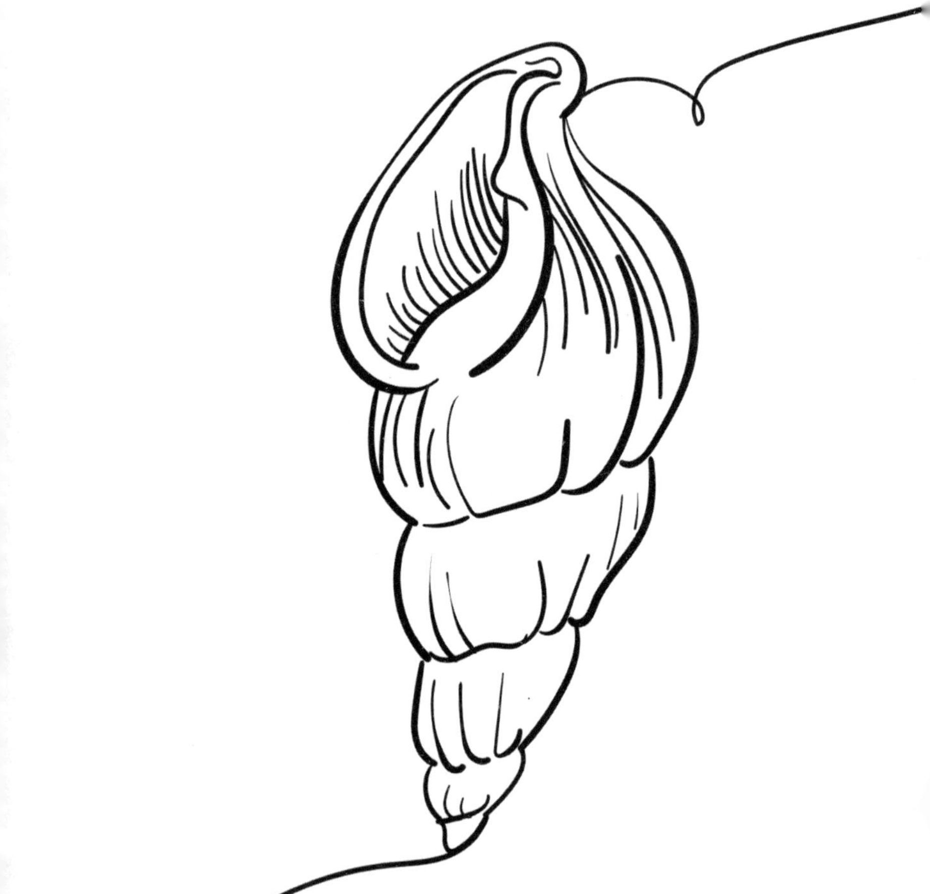

CHAPTER 11
Vermentino

I gazed out onto the wide Southern Ocean. It was a mild spring day. The weather was cool, but the sun shone brightly. The music of the waves was hypnotic. I was happily wrapped in a blanket, seated on a beach towel, with a bottle of water and a container of snacks beside me. Life was good.

I had been pleasantly surprised when Matt had invited me and Mike to join him and the family at a holiday house in Cape Bridgewater. Situated along Victoria's ambling southern coastline, Cape Bridgewater is a secluded stretch of beach and cliffs, forged from the remains of a long-dead volcano. Like the Strathbogie Ranges, it echoes the prehistoric violence of the Earth. Also like the Strathbogie Ranges, Cape Bridgewater is strangely and harshly beautiful. It made sense that this was Matt's home away from home.

'I need more yin in my life,' he said. I was glad this realisation had come to him. 'We're planning on doing as little as possible.'

It sounded perfect to me. Unfortunately, Mike hadn't been able to join us. He was booked out for the next two weeks with the Czech and Slovak Film Festival. There were few things my husband enjoyed as much as indulging in a marathon of obscure cinema.

Yin is what Matt needed and yin is what Matt got. On holiday, his family shifted to a slower gear. There was an aura of joyful calm about the place. Our hours were spent playing games, going for walks, listening to music, talking and napping. All this was done without a single aim in mind, aside from the simple enjoyment of life.

It was on my third day there that I stole away for a couple of hours of solitary reading on the beach. I wanted to give Matt's gang some time 'guest-free'. I also wanted to read.

I was happily lost at sea with Coleridge when I realised someone was approaching.

'I come bearing wine!' Matt announced. He was holding a bottle in one hand and two champagne flutes in the other.

'Thank you!' I said, reaching for my bookmark. 'But where are Lu and the girls?'

'They all went down for a nap after you left. While they're out of action, I thought I would take the opportunity to introduce you to vermentino.'

Matt plonked himself down next to me. 'What are you reading?' he asked.

I showed him the front cover. 'It's about Dionysus, the Greek god of wine,' I told him. 'Our lessons have inspired me to do some background reading into the mythologies surrounding wine.'

I had not told Matt, but when I purchased his statuette of Demeter, I had considered including Dionysus. I thought that pairing the Mother of Agriculture with the Father of Wine would make a perfect present. However, almost every statue of Dionysus I found featured the god bearing a prominent erection. Even when his private parts weren't exposed, Dionysus was depicted with rippling abs. He was made to resemble a gay pin-up model. I decided to just stick with Demeter.

'Have you learnt anything interesting from the book?' he asked.

'Many things. Actually, there's a myth I wanted to share with you.'

I explained that there were several stories concerning the birth of Dionysus. One of the most famous was the myth of Zagreus. According to this account, the god Zeus had a child with the goddess Persephone – the daughter of Demeter. The child's name was Zagreus. Zeus planned for his son Zagreus to become his successor as ruler of the gods. However, Zeus's wife Hera grew jealous of her husband's affair with Persephone. Hera incited the primordial gods – the Titans – to murder Zagreus. The Titans tore Zagreus limb from limb and ate his flesh. Fortunately, Zeus was able to retrieve Zagreus's heart. Zeus used the heart to impregnate the mortal priestess Semele. Semele gave birth to Dionysus, the god of wine, theatre, fertility and revelry. Thus, Zagreus was reborn.

'I thought that myth was a perfect metaphor for winemaking,' I said. 'Just like Dionysus, wine has two mothers.'

Matt raised his right eyebrow, wordlessly requesting a further explanation.

'Dionysus's first mother was Persephone, who was a goddess of nature,' I said. 'Wine's first mother is Mother Nature. She gives birth to the vines and grapes. Dionysus's second mother was a mortal woman. She restored him to life after he was torn to pieces. Likewise, the winemaker is the second mother of wine. The winemaker nurtures and cultivates the wine after the grapes are picked and crushed.'

'I've never thought of myself as a mother before!' Matt said.

'No, I don't imagine many people would think of you as a mother,' I replied, smiling at my friend in his flannel shirt and oilskin vest. His holiday stubble was on the verge of turning into a beard. 'Then again, if the winemaker isn't the mother of wine, who is?'

'You've got me there.' Matt grabbed the bottle next to him. 'Well, as a mother, let me introduce you to one of my children.'

This wine was one of Matt's, but it didn't look like the others we had shared. Instead of a screw-top, it had a ridged metal top. I asked Matt why.

'This is called a "crown seal",' he said, tapping the lid with his index finger. 'Because this is a sparkling wine, we use this seal to lock in the wine's freshness.'

'Why not use a champagne cork?'

'For the same reason we use screw-tops instead of corks for our still wine – we find there's less variation bottle to bottle, and there's no risk of cork taint.'

'"Cork taint"?' The term sounded slightly obscene.

'Corks can sometimes cause unwanted tastes or aromas. Using metal tops eliminates that problem. In fact, it was Australian wineries that led the way in the large-scale adoption of screw-tops and crown seals. A lot of important innovations in the wine industry have come out of Australia.'

Producing a bottle opener from his pocket, Matt opened the wine with a quiet 'pop'. A whisp of gas escaped from the mouth of the bottle, disappearing into the air.

'I'm excited to try our first sparkling white wine together,' I said.

'I'll hazard a guess you've never drunk a sparkling wine quite like this before. Unlike most sparkling whites, this one is made with vermentino grapes.'

Matt handed me my glass. Columns of tiny bubbles moved exuberantly through the pale, straw-coloured wine.

'How do you make wine sparkle?' I asked. This question had never occurred to me before. I had always taken champagne bubbles for granted.

'The mass-market approach is to carbonate the wine like Coca-Cola. It's literally blasted with bubbles. But the traditional method is what's called "secondary fermentation".

This is where the already fermented still wine undergoes another round of fermentation. Sugar and yeast are added, and the wine is fermented in either a tank or the wine bottle itself. This process creates a pressurised environment which causes carbon dioxide bubbles to appear in the wine.'

We proceeded to smell and taste. The wine had the aroma of lemon citrus blossom, and the flavour of Granny Smith apples.

Matt explained that vermentino is an Italian grape whose name was said to derive from the word 'fermento' – meaning 'ferment' or 'yeast'. It is mostly used to make a dry white table wine.

'It grows well in hot climates too,' he said. 'And with the climate heating up, we thought it would be a good one for us to throw into the mix.'

But while Matt was preparing his winery for a warming world, it seemed the vermentino wasn't quite ready for the Strathbogie Ranges. 'Ours is still a relatively cool place to grow wine,' he said. 'We found that our vermentino grapes had difficulty ripening. They retained a lot of acid.'

I picked up a container of mixed nuts that I'd brought with me, and offered it to Matt. I wished I had also brought some strawberries. As I had learnt from *Pretty Woman*, strawberries were the go-to pairing for sparkling white wine.

'Because of vermentino's insane acid retention,' Matt continued, 'it wasn't really working the way we had originally hoped. After getting to know the grape better and understanding how it responded to our climate, we thought: why not try vermentino as a sparkling wine? It was something I never would have considered before. To my knowledge, it had never been done.'

I took a sip. 'How would you say it turned out?'

'It ticked a lot of boxes for restaurants that like niche wines. Our vermentino has also sold better as a sparkling wine than as a table wine. We think it makes a great sparkling wine. But I'll put that question back to you. How would you say it turned out?'

I took another sip. The wine was crisp and fresh, and the bubbles danced on my palate. 'I would say it turned out well.'

Matt smiled and clinked his glass to mine. He was pleased to have earned my tick of approval. Ever the wine egalitarian, my friend valued even my naive opinion.

'I'm interested to hear you talk about getting to know the grape,' I remarked. 'It's almost as if you and the vine are communicating.'

Matt replied with a nod. 'We find the best results come when we listen to the plant and respond to what it's telling us.'

'You're like modern-day shamans,' I suggested.

Once more, Matt raised a questioning eyebrow.

'Shamanism is a big part of indigenous cultures all over the world,' I explained. 'Although it's a fairly broad term, the defining feature of shamanism is communication between our human realm and the non-human realm of animals, plants and spirits.'

'I'm assuming you don't mean spirits as in hard liquor?' said Matt with a wink.

I rolled my eyes. 'Nice dad joke. Anyway, shamans are traditionally mediators between the physical and the spiritual; performing such functions as predicting the future, healing the sick, or placing curses on enemies. But hearing you talk about the connection you develop with the grapevines, I can't help think there is something shamanic about being a winemaker.'

Matt had a curious look on his face. 'I suppose mediating between plants and humans is essentially what a winemaker does,' he said. 'We learn the language of the grapevines and translate it into something that people can understand and enjoy.'

'So, would you say that you're fluent in grapevine?'

'Not at all! It'll take me a lifetime to learn that language. After almost fifteen years as a winemaker, I'd say I'm just getting a handle on the grammar.'

Fifteen years to understand the basics? Not even Chinese is that difficult!

'I assume you know really seasoned winemakers who understand the language well?' I said.

'Absolutely. But the best winemakers don't boast about it. They generally show a lot of humility and deference. They spend their days quietly listening to the grapevines and responding in kind. It's a wonderful thing.'

I turned back to the ocean. My eyes rested on the perpetually moving perimeter between sea and shore – approaching and retreating, approaching and retreating.

'Do you know what the word "liminal" means?' I asked.

Matt shook his head.

'It comes from the Latin "limen", which means "threshold". Liminality is the state of being in-between or in the process of transition. In anthropology, liminal space is the ambiguous region between the known and the unknown.' I motioned towards the shoreline. 'In a sense, the beach is a liminal space. It marks the boundary between our everyday world as land-dwelling humans, and the mysterious depths of the ocean.'

We gazed and sipped some more, the tang of the wine blending with the sea air.

'Dionysus was a liminal deity,' I said. 'He dwelt on the precipice between life and death, light and darkness, mortality and divinity, serenity and insanity. He was a truly ambiguous figure. He was a shapeshifter who could transform himself into anything he wished. In fact, one of his names was Dionysus Polymorphous, or "Dionysus of many forms".'

Matt scratched his chin. 'Like the many forms of wine?'

'Exactly! It makes perfect sense that Dionysus is the god of wine. Especially now that I know how mercurial wine can be, and how it appears in countless variations. I've also been thinking about how wine works as a gateway between different states of mind ...'

'As in sober to not sober?' he offered, with another wink.

'Among other things. Wine is a liminal commodity in more ways than one. But speaking with you now, it occurs to me that the winemaker might be just as liminal as the wine itself.'

Matt took a quick taste from his glass. 'Because we stand at the midpoint between the grapevine and the wine consumer?'

'Sure, but it's more than that. Take you, for example. Your winery sits on the borderline between modern civilisation and a stark, ancient landscape. You use cutting-edge technology alongside centuries-old techniques. You cultivate your wine in wide, open countryside and in a dark, cloistered barrel hall. What you do is somewhere between farming and a refined art form. The list goes on.'

'It's all true,' my friend agreed. 'You've taught me two things about myself today – I'm a mother and I'm liminal!'

'Happy to help!' We raised our glasses and drank a toast. Reaching for my snacks, I was mildly concerned to find we were all out. Being near the ocean always made me ravenously hungry.

Matt provided a timely distraction. 'Mate, look,' he said, pointing out to sea. It was far away and difficult to make out, but there was no doubt something there – a sign of life arising from the vast expanse.

'Is it a seal?' I asked. Cape Bridgewater is well known as a seal-watching spot. It's home to Australia's largest mainland seal colony.

'I think it might be a dolphin,' he replied. I squinted. Was that a dorsal fin? Maybe. Then again, it might be a seal's flipper. We fell silent. A minute or two elapsed as we waited to see the creature more clearly. But it was gone.

'I'd put my money on it being a dolphin,' he said.

'It would be fitting if it was,' I said. 'Our old wine god Dionysus was closely associated with dolphins.'

I recounted the tale of Dionysus being abducted by pirates. They had mistaken Dionysus for a wealthy prince and kidnapped him in the hope of receiving a large ransom. Enraged by their impertinence, Dionysus transformed himself into a ferocious lion. He also transformed the oars of their ship into snakes. Terrified, the pirates threw themselves overboard. Taking pity on the men, Dionysus saved them from drowning by turning them into dolphins – creatures that the ancient Greeks viewed as altruistic, as they were known to aid sailors in peril. Thus, Dionysus changed the pirates from violent criminals into helpful sea mammals.

'I've heard that before – that dolphins sometimes rescue people who are drowning or help fishermen to catch fish,' said Matt. 'It's strange given how bloody awful humans can be to animals.'

I'd had the same thought when reading about the kindly nature of dolphins – why help humans? Of all the species on Earth, aren't we the most dangerous and destructive? It was hard not to feel misanthropic when I considered the enormous calamities that humans had inflicted on the natural world. Evidently, dolphins are not in the business of holding grudges.

'It's something we've really lost sight of in our modern world – the way humans and animals can support one another,' said Matt. 'In the vineyard, we go out of our way to protect spiders and ladybirds because they help to keep pestilence at bay. This makes the vineyard look fairly rough and woolly at times, but we want weeds and different plant varieties to grow as homes for the insects. We know that if we look after them, they'll look after us.'

A fresh round of happy bubbles filled my glass.

'Most people,' Matt said, 'are grossed out if they get a spiderweb caught on them. But I get excited. It means that the spiders are doing their job. I often say "thank you" in my mind when I see a spider or a ladybird.'

I recalled a line attributed to the 13th-century Christian mystic Meister Eckhart: 'If the only prayer you ever say in your entire life is "thank you", it will be enough.' Matt's grateful ways with the natural world certainly weren't the norm these days.

'For most of us,' I said, 'our entire lives are set up to keep nature out of the way.'

Matt shook his head sadly. 'The thing is, I don't find my connection with nature that remarkable. What I find remarkable is that so many people *don't* share a connection with nature. I saw a study suggesting that a third of kids don't know that milk comes from cows. That's mind-boggling!'

I looked down at my feet. I felt guilty. I could hardly boast a strong connection with nature myself – at most, it was a work in progress.

'Why do you think we've become so disconnected from nature?' Matt asked. I was reminded of Lilli asking me why there was war. It was a complicated question.

'I think a lot of it comes down to the way we view our world,' I said. 'The prevalent modern view says that anything which isn't human is simply a resource. The natural world lacks any value of its own. It is only assigned value when it becomes useful to human beings.'

I picked up a small opalescent shell; one of three I'd collected on the beach that morning.

'By contrast, it is common for cultures that revere nature to hold an animistic world view. According to animism, everything has a spiritual dimension. This means that animals, plants, trees, mountains, rivers, stones, shells – all things in nature – have their own spirit and their own value.'

I turned the iridescent shell over in my hand.

'Putting aside the question of whether everything actually possesses a soul or not, it makes sense that animism would go hand in hand with a respectful and reciprocal attitude towards nature. Which is interesting, because I find the way you speak about nature distinctly animistic.'

Matt took a sip before speaking. 'I don't view myself as an overly spiritual person, but I guess that's true. I tend to think of the different grapevine varieties as having different personalities.'

I had been delighted before by the way Matt personified his grapevines. It was more than just a charming way of describing things. 'I love that the grapevines are like family members to you,' I said.

'They really are,' he said. 'Come to think of it, in the vineyard we often discuss the grapevines in terms of their emotions – this vine is feeling happy, this one is feeling grumpy. When you spend enough time with the vines, you get a sense of their different moods. It seems completely natural in the vineyard. But talking about it now, I don't know ... is it weird?'

I laughed. 'I am definitely the wrong person to judge whether something is weird or not. But no, I don't think so. I imagine if you were to discuss the matter with a shaman, they would think it was incredibly weird to *not* talk about the moods and personalities of plants.'

I was about to mention that in ancient Greece, grapevines were considered the physical embodiment of Dionysius – the god's spirit was believed to live in the grapes and their wine. But I didn't get a chance. I heard a little girl's voice ring out: 'Daddy!'

We turned to see Matt's daughters running along the beach towards us. Lu was close behind, looking peaceful and fresh after her nap. As always, Matt's face lit up at the sight of his family.

'Time to wrap up,' I said, downing the last of my vermentino.

I gathered up the shells I had collected. My plan was to give one to each of Matt's daughters. But now I couldn't decide which shell to give to which girl. I'd have to let them decide. Or perhaps I should let the shells decide for themselves?

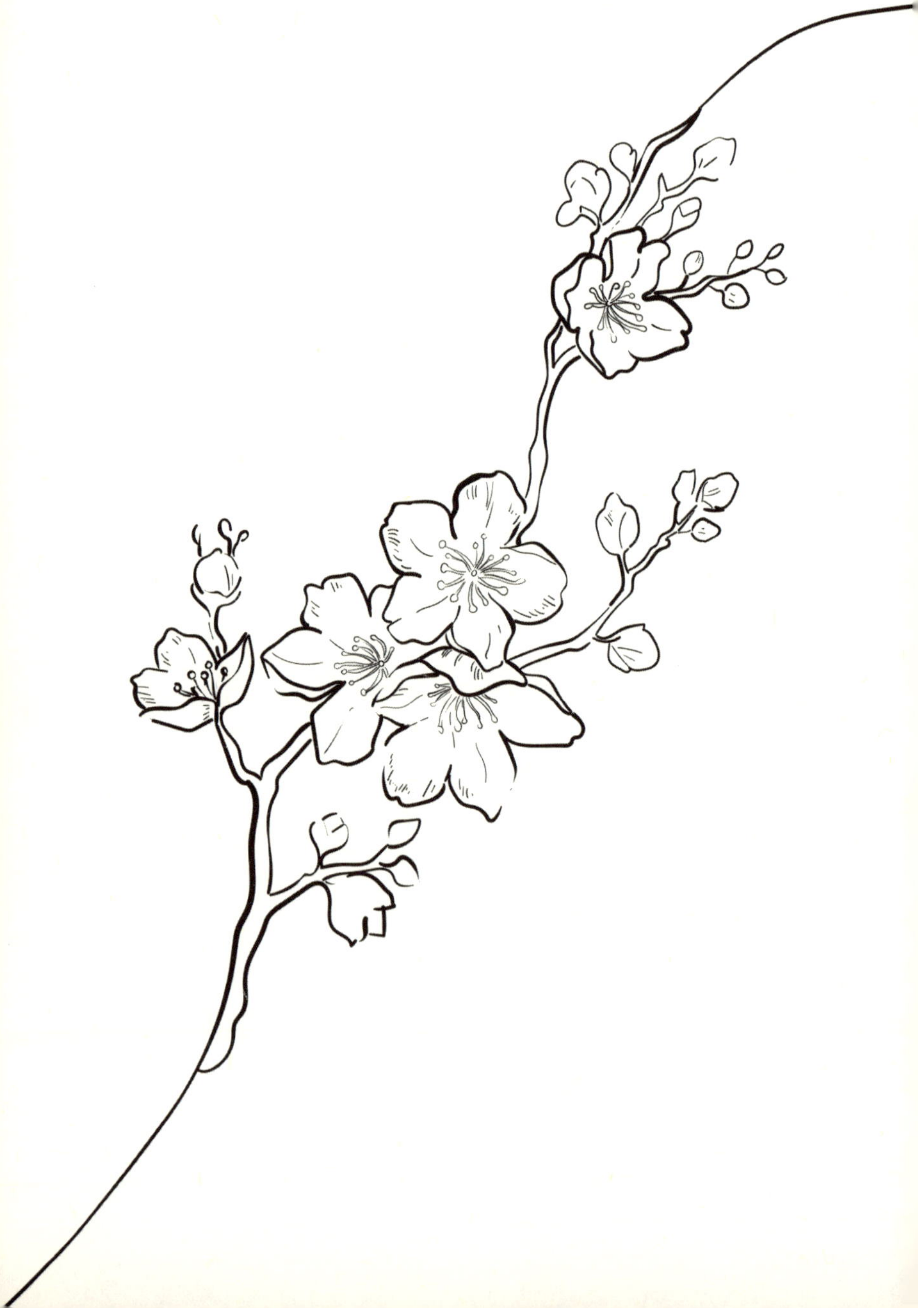

CHAPTER 12
Sauvignon Blanc

'To quote Agent Cooper from *Twin Peaks*, this is a damn fine cup of coffee,' I said, resting my mug on the grey ironbark railing beside me.

Matt and I were sitting on the deck of the holiday house at Cape Bridgewater. A flock of seagulls hovered above the ocean, hanging in the air like ornaments on a string mobile. The wind and the waves and the caws of the gulls made the ideal soundtrack for our mid-morning respite. It was the final day of our holiday.

'That coffee was made with love,' he replied. I turned to my friend and smiled. He had changed noticeably since the beginning of the holiday. The tension had disappeared from his face. He looked healthy and well rested. His eyes twinkled. Even the tone of his voice had mellowed.

'So, what's our next wine?' I asked. 'And when should we try it?'

Matt pondered for a moment. 'I'd love to introduce you to nebbiolo. Afterwards, we could try gamay and grüner veltliner. There's a whole world for us to explore. But I have a bottle of sauvignon blanc to share.'

After all those strange wine names, I was content that our next wine was in the realm of the familiar. I'd at least heard of sauvignon blanc. The other names were totally foreign to me. They sounded more like astronomical phenomena than wine varieties. It was easy to imagine the 'nebbiolo galaxy' or the 'gamay nebula' or the 'grüner veltliner asteroid belt'. I didn't even know which were red and which were white. I still had so much to learn.

As for when we'd sample that sauvignon blanc, well, that was where the yang came back into Matt's schedule.

'Things are looking hectic for a while,' he said. The innumerable demands of running a winery awaited him. 'I was thinking when I woke up this morning about everything I've got to do when I get back. Even next week's going to be insane. Along with all the usual stuff, I have a two-day wine seminar in the Yarra Valley next weekend.'

My ears pricked at the mention of the Yarra Valley. I had always wanted to visit Victoria's renowned wine region in the springtime. Every year I meant to go, and every year I had failed to. Pulling out my phone, I did a quick search. The timing would be perfect for something else I had in mind.

'How about we meet in the Yarra Valley next weekend for a picnic?' I proposed.

'Don't you have work to catch up on?'

'I do, but the Yarra Valley Cherry Blossom Festival is on next week!' I could hardly contain my excitement. 'I can always do work, but I can't always see cherry blossoms!'

With a laugh, Matt agreed to escape the seminar for a lunchtime sojourn in a cherry orchard.

I insisted that I would organise the food for a change. 'But what would I make to pair with sauvignon blanc?'

'Scallop ceviche would be perfect,' Matt said.

I shot my friend a wilting glance. 'That would be a "no". If I try to make a raw seafood dish, we'll end up in the hospital.'

He chuckled. 'Would chicken sandwiches with mayonnaise and chives be doable?'

'It's a deal! I'll bring the food, you bring the wine, and Mother Nature will bring the blossoms.'

Dame Nature more than held up her end of the bargain. The blossoms were enchanting. As Matt and I strolled around the orchard surrounded by clouds of pink petals, it was impossible not to marvel at her talents. We weren't the only ones, of course. The orchard's corridors bustled with visitors. Small children squealed with excitement. Couples held hands and kissed. Pensioners quietly wandered. Everywhere there were signs of happiness.

'Coming here was a great idea,' said Matt. 'Life doesn't get much better than this.'

'It really doesn't.' I was absorbed in gazing at a particularly lovely tree. Its elegant posture, and the flourish of its blossoms, spoke to me. If Matt had not been with me, I might have sat down and stared at it for an hour. I wished I knew a suitable haiku to encapsulate the tree's rare beauty. Unfortunately, I had never learnt the verses of the great Japanese poets. I was haiku-less.

After walking for a while, we found a secluded spot to set up base. I laid out a picnic blanket, crockery, glassware and food. We made ourselves comfortable on the blanket. Matt reached into his cooler bag and produced our bottle of wine. We were underway.

'Sauvignon blanc is a really fun wine,' he said as he opened the bottle. 'It's not one I'd typically build a menu around. It's more of a wine you'd enjoy at a spa day or during a night out on the town.'

'Or on a picnic in a cherry blossom orchard,' I added.

'One hundred per cent.' He filled our glasses. 'The pleasure of sauvignon blanc lies in its simplicity. We're not looking for layers or subtlety with this one.'

I smelt it. The aroma was forthright and unmistakable. 'Wow! It's like putting a freshly opened passionfruit right under your nose!'

'Spot on. There are other tropical fruit aromas like pawpaw and melon in there, but passionfruit is the most obvious for sure.'

'Obvious' was the right word. Despite its negative connotations, there were many things I enjoyed which were 'obvious' – fireworks, the Spice Girls, beehive hairdos. 'Obvious' was not always a bad thing. 'Obvious' could be spectacular.

I took my first sip. 'Mmm ... that's delightful.'

'Delicious, isn't it?' he said proudly. 'You really get that tropical fruit flavour. There's also citrus in there, which helps to give it that clean finish.'

I took another effortless sip. This was the kind of wine that could disappear quickly. I made a mental note not to glug the entire glass in five minutes.

'Everything about this wine is easy,' I observed. 'It's easy to appreciate and it's easy to drink.'

'It's also got that "wow" factor, which we just saw in your reaction to the aroma. I think of sauvignon blanc as a beautiful, blonde bombshell.'

'Or it might be a drag queen covered in feathers and diamantés, lip-syncing to Diana Ross?' The drag queen I had in mind was wearing a Carmen-Miranda-style headpiece made entirely of tropical fruits. Utterly bold, entirely shameless, and completely fabulous.

Matt chuckled. 'That works as well. Either way, it's easy to see why sauvignon blanc has become an international superstar over the past couple of decades.'

I cast my mind back to our session with chardonnay, that other 'easy to enjoy' white. The popularity of these wines, I concluded, had something to do with people seeking solace in simplicity. It's only human to opt for something uncomplicated in a fast-paced, complex world. Although I had no real insight into the driving forces behind wine market trends, there was psychological symmetry to it all. These wines 'paired' with the feeling of the time.

'Tell me more about wine pairing,' I said, reaching for the container of sandwiches. 'For example, why do scallop ceviche, or chicken sandwiches, work well with sauvignon blanc?'

'Those two are excellent examples of how food pairing can be either complementary or contrasting,' Matt replied. 'Scallop ceviche is made with citrus juice. It's an acid-fresh dish that complements an acid-fresh wine like sauvignon blanc. Chicken sandwiches with sauvignon blanc is a pairing based on contrast. The mayonnaise is fatty, so the acid in the wine cuts through the fat and freshens the palate. The contrast creates balance.'

I placed the sandwiches onto the plates and handed one to Matt.

'It seems to me that the same applies when it comes to pairing wine with occasions,' I said. 'For example, sparkling white wine pairs well with celebrations because it complements them. The wine is bubbly and joyful, just like any good party should be. But I can also see myself reaching for a bottle of sparkling vermentino to give me a boost after a crappy day of work.'

As Matt chewed, he gave me a thumbs up. My amateur gourmet skills had paid off. He washed it down with a gulp of wine.

'Wine can be like cake that way,' he said. 'You might eat cake at a birthday party or you might have it as comfort food after you've been dumped. Complement and contrast.'

I began tucking into a sandwich. As I finished my first mouthful, I took a sip, paying close attention to the sauvignon blanc's flavour and feeling.

'I can see what you mean,' I said. 'It's like a spoon of lemon sorbet in the middle of a degustation.'

I took another sip and found that my glass was empty. I had failed in my exercise of self-restraint. Without a word, Matt recharged my glass.

'So,' I said, 'just as the same wine might be paired with two entirely different occasions, my guess is that two entirely different wines could be paired with the same occasion.'

Matt looked intrigued. 'Go on.'

'Say you're having a deep and meaningful conversation with someone close to you. You could pair the moment with a complex wine variety like pinot noir to complement the mood. But you could also share a fun and approachable wine like sauvignon blanc as an antidote to the discussion's emotional heaviness.'

'I think that's right,' he said. 'You know, before the Cape Bridgewater holiday I was getting fairly burnt out. There was one day when I just had to take a break. I went to the cellar and picked out an expensive bottle of Burgundian chardonnay. I wanted something layered and nuanced to contrast with the hack and grind of working life. That chardonnay gave me the most pleasant and meandering experience. It was the perfect antidote for how I'd been feeling.'

From yang to yin in a single bottle.

'You paired the wine with your state of mind to create balance,' I observed.

'People who know wine can do that. They can intuit which bottle to open when they need comfort or a pick-me-up. It's because they understand the character of the wine.'

'Why don't winemakers and sommeliers recommend wines to pair with different moods?' I asked. 'It's something wine novices would probably find useful.'

'As in, "if you're feeling sad, try this merlot" or, "if you're feeling creative, try this shiraz"?'

I nodded with gusto. I had just popped a sizeable amount of sandwich in my mouth. Any attempt to speak would have emerged as a mayonnaise-flavoured mumble.

'Sounds interesting!' said Matt. 'Of course, there's a specific science behind food and wine pairing. Working out a science behind *mood* and wine pairing might prove challenging.'

He was right. Pinning down the experiences of the heart was a tricky business. Emotions inhabited a landscape of shades, enigmas and contradictions. I had always believed that artists like Marc Chagall or Edvard Munch did a better job of capturing human feeling than any scientist could. I recalled the words of the author Thomas Hardy: 'Poetry is emotion put into measure. The emotion must come by nature, but the measure can be acquired by art.'

We fell silent as we continued to eat our sandwiches and drink our wine. I watched petals flutter from a tree nearby. In a week or so, all the blossoms would be gone, and the seasons would continue to turn.

'So,' Matt said, pointing to my almost empty glass, 'you've had two glasses of sauvignon blanc now. What do you think? Have you joined the world and fallen in love?'

I took a moment to reflect on my remaining share of wine. Sight, smell and taste. I quickly swirled the glass before bringing it to my lips. I finished it off in one sip.

'I don't know if I'm in love with sauvignon blanc, but I do love its simplicity,' I said. 'Once again, my mind goes to Taoism. The Taoist philosophers say that the true sage is free from any pretence. They have returned to their most simple and natural way of being. The Taoists talk about "Pu".'

'Poo?'

'No, "*Pu*", spelt with a "p" and a "u",' I corrected, as Matt stifled a laugh. '"Pu" is translated as "uncarved wood", which is a metaphor the Taoists use to describe the inborn simplicity of the sage. It is this simplicity that gives sages their strength. Sauvignon blanc reminds me of that.'

Matt drank the last of his wine. 'Strength and simplicity are perfect words for sauvignon blanc. You wouldn't necessarily think those two things go together, but it's the wine's simplicity that gives it its confidence.'

'Those Taoist philosophers knew what they were talking about,' I said.

We were done with our wine and sandwiches, but I had also prepared a dessert.

'How do you feel about baked cheesecake?' I asked. Matt confirmed that he was strongly in favour. Plucking the container from the picnic basket, I served our second course.

'Nice one, mate!' Matt said as I passed him his plate. 'But before we get stuck in, is there anything else you'd like to discuss about sauvignon blanc? Any questions or observations?'

I wanted to keep talking. The sharing of thoughts was an endless pursuit of mine. But what more was there to be said about sauvignon blanc? Its nature spoke for itself. No amount of talking would make its simplicity complex or give its boldness any depth.

The wisdom of the Taoists lay not only in what they said, but also in what they did not say. The very first verse of the *Tao Te Ching* taught that the true nature of reality – the Tao – could not be described. The moment it was hemmed in with words, the description of the Tao became incomplete. To define the Tao in language was to say what it was, and what it was not. But the Tao could not be defined in reference to anything else. It transcended all confines of human understanding. For this reason, a true sage spoke little. They embodied their wisdom in silence.

I would have made a terrible Taoist sage.

'You know what,' I said, grasping my cake fork. 'I don't think I've got anything more to say. How do you feel about just eating cake and watching the cherry blossoms with me?'

'I would love to,' my friend replied.

Epilogue
The Unopened Bottle

> 'We shall not cease from exploration, and the end of
> all our exploring will be to arrive where we started and
> know the place for the first time.'
>
> – TS Eliot

Once again, I was back in a bottle shop, grabbing something nice. As I entered, I was stopped by a moment of recognition. The man behind the counter looked familiar. But who was he? He was tall and broad. He had a handsome face, framed by a tidy beard. The answer dawned on me.

'You're Dale from the wine bar,' I said.

'And you're Matt Fowles's friend?'

I shook his hand and reintroduced myself. In the time since we'd first met, Dale had passed his Advanced Sommelier exam, left the wine bar and opened his own shop. Things were going well.

'I remember Matt saying he was teaching you about wine,' he said. 'How are the lessons going?'

'Really well,' I replied. 'In fact, I'm here to buy a bottle of nebbiolo for that very reason. Matt gave me the task of choosing the wine. It feels like a test.'

'Let's make sure you don't fail. Do you have any specific nebbiolos in mind?'

I handed Dale my short list. He glanced it over. 'I believe we have one of these in stock, but I'll have to check out the back.'

Alone in the store, I surveyed my surroundings. Glowing refrigerators of white wines, and shelves replete with reds, offered an embarrassment of riches. I eagerly set about exploring the aisles.

Beautifully designed labels boasted names from around the world – old world, new world, and every world in between. Burgundian pinot noir and Italian sangiovese cohabited with Algerian cinsault and Georgian saperavi. I examined well-travelled bottles and wondered: what would it be like to taste a chardonnay made in the Shanxi province of China, or a cabernet grown in the south of Lebanon? The varieties, blends, vintages, wineries, regions and countries were apparently endless. How could anyone ever become a genuine 'Master of Wine'? Who could possibly fathom the depths of such a vast and ever-changing universe?

I turned to see Dale standing next to me. 'I'm really sorry,' he said, 'but it looks like I don't have any of the nebbiolos on your list.'

'That's okay,' I said cheerfully. 'You have such an amazing range. I'm sure you can find me the perfect nebbiolo among what you have here.'

'Absolutely!' Dale charged off and I followed quickly behind. At the opposite end of the store, he abruptly stopped and pulled a bottle from a shelf. It was Matt's shiraz.

'Did Matt get you to taste this one?' he asked.

'He did. In fact, that was the wine he had me try in our very first lesson.'

'He started you off well,' Dale replied.

Plucking out a bottle of Yarra Valley nebbiolo, he began extolling its virtues – the ripe cherry aroma, powdery tannins, and 'grip'. I struggled to pay attention. My thoughts were elsewhere. At the sight of Matt's shiraz, memories of our afternoon at the 'grand ravine' came flooding back. The sound of birds and rippling stream water mingled with the smell of fresh air and gum trees. Images of whirling dervishes and Vermeer paintings passed my mind's eye. I remembered poetry and curiosity and surprise. Then there was the wine itself – violets, plums and purples.

Dale was handing me the bottle. 'There are a few more I could recommend, but I think this is your best bet for impressing Matt.'

I looked over the bottle's label and smiled. 'I'm happy to buy this one. The bonus of going with your choice is that if the wine's no good, it's not my fault!'

He laughed. 'Anything else you're after?'

I considered the question. Should I purchase a kindly merlot or a rascally arneis? Was there a wise cabernet or a flamboyant sauvignon blanc with my name on it?

'It's tempting, but no thanks,' I said. 'If I start, I won't know where to stop. There are just so many wines. Don't you ever find it overwhelming?'

'Not at all,' Dale countered with a smile. 'I love that there's always something new to try. I get more excited by the bottles I haven't opened than the ones I have.'

The unopened bottle. That was where the wonder was. And what was the point of wine if not to create wonder?

'Which wines has Matt taught you about?' Dale asked as we returned to the cash register. One by one, I listed them, telling anecdotes as I went. With the name of each wine came recollections of flavours and feelings so vivid I could hardly tell where the past ended and the present began. I spoke of Taoist philosophy and shamanic mythology, Marcel Proust and Virginia Woolf, the god Dionysus and Indra's net – the full peacock's tail.

'Wow!' Dale said. 'It sounds like your lessons roamed far and wide.'

He handed me the nebbiolo and I held it gently. I thought of the hours shared with Matt. I thought of the conversations, the laughter, and the silences. Most of all, I thought of the friendship.

It was true. My weekends with Matt had been about so much more than wine.

Acknowledgements

Peter

It goes without saying that there would be no *Weekends with Matt* without my good friend Matt Fowles. You are a kind, determined, gentle, resilient and thoughtful man. Thank you for the years of friendship, hours of conversation, your hospitality and unwavering belief in me. I love you, buddy.

Thank you, thank you, thank you Rosemary Moore. I don't know how you managed to do all those transcriptions without losing your mind, but we're so grateful you did! You deserve a lifetime supply of vegan treats.

I owe an enormous debt of gratitude to Paul Tavatgis. Your reassurance and thoughtful feedback helped me more than I can say. You are a fabulous friend.

We were incredibly fortunate to have the advocacy and inspiration of wine critic, novelist and bon vivant Campbell Mattinson. Your generous support has meant the world.

A massive shout-out to our publishing fairy godmother Roxy Ryan. To me you will always be a combination of Mary Poppins, Grace Coddington and Wonder Woman. Your persistence paid off and we can never thank you enough.

HUGE thanks to Martin Hughes for putting the full force of your considerable passion behind this book and thank you Mic Looby for your brilliant and considered edits – you are the champions. Thank you also to Ruby Ashby-Orr, Grace Breen, Rosanna Hunt, Susie Kennewell, Keiran Rogers and the entire gang at Affirm Press. We couldn't have wished for a better publishing team.

Thank you Karen Wallis of Taloula Press for your illustrations and cover art. You did a stunning job.

Many thanks to all those kind and patient souls who read excerpts, listened to ideas, and provided encouragement along the way. Specifically, I want to thank Brock Bastian, Stephen Bordignon, Emma Collingwood, Kane Ford, Matthew Giulieri, Carol Hagan, Simon Hendel, Ben Holgate, Christopher Jackson, Ethan Keogh, Emma Langridge, Candice Parr, Gavin Smith, Gareth Simpson and Peter Young.

I extend endless thanks and love to Anna Achia, Nicola Hogan and Denise Parsons. You know what you did.

The biggest thank you goes to my husband, Mike. Words fail me, so I will borrow the words of our favourite Turkish novelist Elif Shafak: 'Love cannot be explained. It can only be experienced. Love cannot be explained, yet it explains all.' As I've told you many times, you're the best husband in the whole wide world.

Matt

To my wonderful wife, Luise, thanks for your love, unending support and for the gentle guidance you give our girls each day. I am so happy to be doing this with you. Life with you is fun.

To my beautiful daughters, Lilli, Mathilda and Ella, you fill my heart with joy. I love that every day with you is an adventure. Your incredible imaginations ignite my own.

To Mum and Dad – you work so hard and with such integrity, giving us all an incredible example to follow. You have afforded your children and grandchildren every opportunity, which is surely one of the more meaningful achievements in life. We are forever grateful for your love, interest, generosity and support.

To my brothers, Will, Jim and Jack, thanks for laughing with me, challenging me and sharing this life with me. Happily, there is never a dull moment!

To Jean and Frank, your kindness and patience for our girls, your support of every project we undertake and your legendary hospitality are always greatly appreciated.

To Jess, Jay, Elise, Alexandra and Gene, you are family, but you are also my great mates. I adore the time we have together.

To my mates Willo and Sahhar, you and your beautiful families mean the world to me.

To my cousins, you are the greatest source of laughter in my life. Your humour knows no bounds.

Finally, to Pete ... You are an extraordinary human and I

feel lucky to know you. I have always been attracted to your intelligence and wisdom which shines brightly from you. You have taught me so much.